All the Things We Didn't Say

All the Things We Didn't Say

TWO MEMOIRS

Marion Garrard Barnwell

AND

Mary DuBose Trice Clark

UNIVERSITY PRESS OF MISSISSIPPI / JACKSON

Willie Morris Books in Memoir and Biography

The University Press of Mississippi is the scholarly publishing agency of the Mississippi Institutions of Higher Learning: Alcorn State University, Delta State University, Jackson State University, Mississippi State University, Mississippi University for Women, Mississippi Valley State University, University of Mississippi, and University of Southern Mississippi.

www.upress.state.ms.us

Designed by Peter D. Halverson

The University Press of Mississippi is a member of the Association of University Presses.

Manufactured in the United States of America
∞

Library of Congress Control Number: 2024021577

Hardback ISBN 978-1-4968-5411-7
Epub single ISBN 978-1-4968-5410-0
Epub institutional ISBN 978-1-4968-5412-4
PDF single ISBN 978-1-4968-5413-1
PDF institutional ISBN 978-1-4968-5414-8

British Library Cataloging-in-Publication Data available

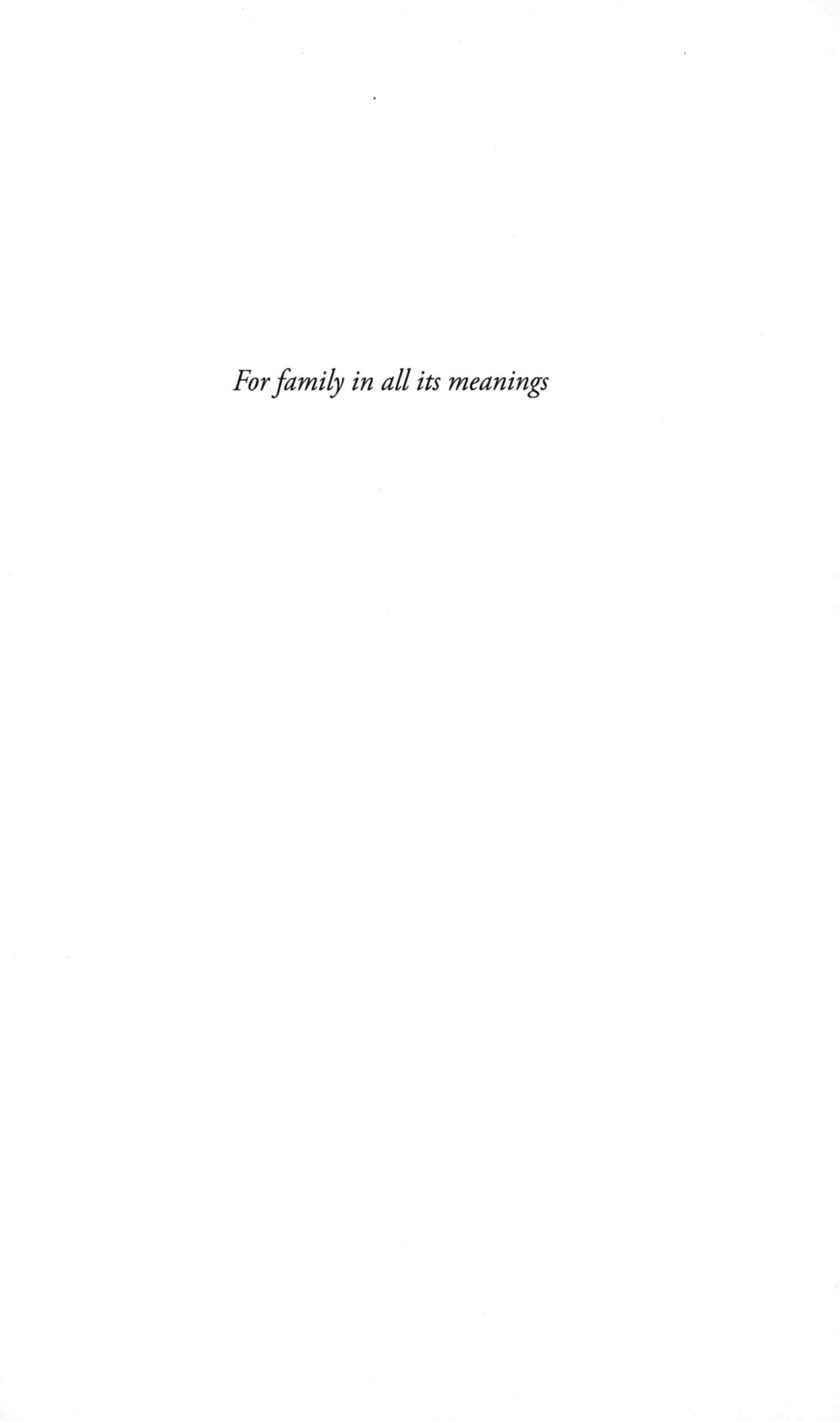

For family in all its meanings

Contents

Acknowledgments

I want to thank Craig Gill, editor in chief at University Press of Mississippi, who overheard me talking to a friend about my idea for a memoir and saw the possibilities. A big thank you to acquisitions editor, Lisa McMurtray, for her astute guidance, and to the staff at University Press of Mississippi who work tirelessly to produce great books. Special thanks to Pete Halverson for producing the beautiful cover art and to project editor Shane Gong Stewart. I am grateful to Gerry Wilson for her time and skill in reading an early draft of my manuscript and Chrissy Wilson for her later edits. A special thank you to my sister Mary for her enthusiasm and valuable suggestions.

To my friends in the writing life who encourage and inspire me: my advocate, Ellen Ann Fentress, my inspiration, Teresa Nicholas, and other fellow writers Susan Ford, Carolyn Elkins, Elizabeth Sarcone, Bill Spencer, Terry Alford, Mike Speer, Patti Carr Black, Lovejoy Boteler, John Floyd, Gerry Helferich, JoAnne Prichard Morris, Libby Hartfield, and Celia Wood. I want to thank Professor Matthew Guinn, who advised me to just do it. I am fortunate to belong to a Dream Group, led by Karen Bonner, that has taught me to listen and respond to my dreams. I am grateful to have in Jackson a great independent bookstore and want to thank owner John Evans for hiring people who love books and for bringing in such outstanding visiting writers.

I hold dear the friends who have gone before me, touchstones along the way: David Clark, Dorothy Shawhan, Sue Stock, Leila Wynn, and Eleanor Failing. Deep appreciation to Jimmy and Cynthia Abbott for a friendship that sustains me. I am indebted to my maternal grandmother whose memoir inspired mine. Mine is a small tribute to her for the many times she put our needs before her own. I am grateful to my sister Mary for her wisdom, enthusiasm, support, suggestions, and our lifelong friendship. I am privileged to have two amazing grandchildren, Joshua and Clai, living reminders of the invaluable link between our generations. I am inspired every day by my children, Craig and Will, who have broken the cycle of addiction in our family. In finding and speaking their truths, they are making unique, authentic, and life-affirming choices that are blessings to us all. My deepest gratitude to my husband, Claiborne, my bridge over troubled waters.

Preface

I didn't know I was going to write a memoir. I thought I was going to write about my maternal grandmother, whom I called Ganny. It was going to be a loving portrait inspired by the memoir she wrote in 1956. I remembered it as a beautiful glimpse of her past, but on rereading it in different circumstances, I became frustrated with all the things she didn't say. She left out everything personal, how she felt about her mother and father, her brothers, her husband, and, most important to me, my mother.

I began to challenge her, in my mind at least. I was curious to know why she stopped her memoir at her marriage in 1900, leaving off the next five decades. I wanted to know not only about parts she left out but also parts she glossed over, many of which I knew about firsthand since she lived with us from just before I was born until she died when I was a junior in college. Family letters and records helped, but I also had to rely on intuition, imagination, and reasonable guesses.

My need to set the record straight and assert my own truths led me to write my own memoir. Once I got started, I wondered what had taken me so long. The memoir form felt natural to me. It allowed me to stay close to my feelings, intuitions, dreams, and messages from the unconscious. After I accepted the challenge of writing it, ideas and answers came to me in mysterious ways.

The disparity between Ganny's memoir and mine indicates how far we humans have come in understanding ourselves, our feelings, and our addictions. It's acceptable for me to talk about family difficulties and dysfunctions that were taboo in the 1950s, a conformist era. Taking a deep look at Ganny's life helped me see the danger in keeping family secrets. In voicing my secrets, I have given them room to breathe, and I see that my problems are not unique.

An old fable that has been told in many ways goes something like this: A man is sitting on a chest by the wayside watching people passing him on foot. To each of them he asks the same question: "Have you seen my treasure?" Days go by, many travelers go past, and he continues to ask the same question until one day a wise old man says, "You're sitting on it." And so he was. All this time he'd been sitting on his chest of treasures.

The chest of treasures is a metaphor for our vast inner resources, but for me it is also literal. I inherited a secretary from my mother that stands in the living room near the front door. On the open shelves at the top are family photographs, a pair of figurines, three gold cups from Japan, and a man's pocket watch under a dome. Below the shelves is a hinged writing desk that folds out.

Beneath the desk are three drawers. One is for my stationery and notebooks. The other two are crammed with letters from my grandfather to my grandmother, from Mother and Daddy to each other, from Mother to my sister, from me to Mother, from Mother to Ganny, and many more from or to cousins, aunts, and uncles. Along with the letters, there are yellowing genealogical charts, dusty monographs, awards, telegrams, curling photographs, certificates, diplomas, and family records.

For over forty years, I walked past this secretary and ignored its contents. My sister and I once tried to read the letters and organize them, but we didn't get very far. When I dared make another attempt, though it was a Pandora's box, I persevered. For many months now, I have been reading, sorting, and responding to these treasures. Along with filling in the gaps in Ganny's memoirs, they have expanded and enriched my memories and widened the net of connections. They have shown me that I'm more than a daughter of two fallible parents and that I am rich in grandparents, aunts, uncles, and cousins.

Because the impulse to write is strong on both sides of my family, I have at my disposal many additional sources that broadened the memoir. Along with my own writings and journals, I have on my shelves ten books and numerous scholarly articles written by my sister and several books, articles, and collections written by various aunts and uncles.

I've organized the book in two parts. Part I is Ganny's memoir, in print for the first time. I have transcribed her handwritten version into a typed form but left it exactly as she wrote it, with nonstandard spellings and punctuation intact. Part I also includes my speculations about her, the subterfuges and subtexts, and my attempts to fill in the gaps. Part II is my memoir, beginning with my forebears, grandparents, parents, and on to my birth and my life up until only a few months ago. I included addenda for items that didn't fit the narrative.

I am fortunate to have access to an understanding of psychology unavailable to Ganny. Therapists, gurus, shamans, priests, poets, and psychologists have informed my understanding of myself and my family. I have read firsthand some of Jung's works and am grateful to have been a member of a dream group for over twenty years based on his study of dreams.

I am deeply grateful to Bill W. and other founders of Alcoholics Anonymous for their understanding of alcoholism. I am grateful every day for the way A. A. has broken the cycle of addiction in my family. Both my parents were unrecovered alcoholics. Both my children are recovering alcoholics who have been clean and sober for over twenty years and counting. Their paths to recovery were remarkable, but those stories are theirs to tell, not mine.

If my children or my grandchildren should read this one day and wish I'd answered one of their burning questions about the family, I hope it sets them on their own quest for understanding their legacy as Ganny's did for me. This is not a tell-all autobiography but a *tell-enough* memoir about a few things significant to me and how they shaped me.

While I was teaching at Delta State University, my fellow teachers and I would talk over lunch about the difficulties of living in Mississippi. After they shared their fantasies about leaving, I'd say, "I'm staying right here where my problems are." I was only partly kidding. I think part of me wanted and needed to stay here in Mississippi, to look at difficulties such as alcoholism and discrimination face on.

In writing the memoir, I've gained a new appreciation and awe at how far women have come since Ganny's time. In thinking about my two Marys, my grandmother and my sister, our progress has been dramatic. Ganny's was a carefully circumscribed life. She made the most of it, but I can imagine her life would have been very different had she lived in our time. My sister is living proof of what is now possible for women. With sensitivity, intelligence, and courage, she has challenged her fellow art historians to include women artists who, throughout history, have been suppressed or ignored.

The physical secretary in my living room represents a lifestyle that we may be losing. Texts and emails can't take the place of sitting at a desk, picking up a pen, and taking the time to compose one's thoughts. Emails and texts can't replace the ritual of putting a letter in an envelope, sealing it, affixing a stamp, and taking it to a mailbox. When I read the letters, say, from my Uncle Cannon to Ganny, he came alive for me in ways I couldn't appreciate as a child.

The geographical landmarks of my mother's childhood in Tupelo and her marriage in Pass Christian are gone—the former blown away by a tornado, the latter by two hurricanes. I might make a symbol of these losses, but a more pressing need is to point out that when landmarks disappear or letters stay unwritten, we lose essential knowledge that helps us see that we are so much more than one particular life.

Prologue

> There's a divinity that shapes our ends
> Rough-hew them how we will.
>
> —WILLIAM SHAKESPEARE

Ganny and I are sitting in her bedroom in two chairs facing each other. I am probably ten, which would make her seventy-six. The house has a lonely Sunday feeling because Annie, our cook, doesn't come on Sundays. Lonely too because my sister has gone off to college.

We hear laughter. It rips through the air and stops our conversation. We avoid each other's eyes. My chest is tight. Ganny's jaw is set. She clutches the armrest with one hand, pleats her skirt with the other.

Their loud voices and raucous laughter travel from the porch, through the library and living room, and down a long hall to Ganny's room at the back of the house. Mother and Daddy are partying with their drinking buddies. We can't unhear them.

I feel betrayed, hurt, and resentful. I can guess from looking at her that Ganny feels those same things, but we are silent.

Part I

Ganny's Memoir

Preview

Here are some brief descriptions of family members important to her memoir:

(A single heart identifies each family member. A double heart signifies immediate family.)

- ♥ *Zachary was Ganny's father whom she calls "Papa." He worked in a mercantile business and as a bookkeeper.*
- ♥ *Anna Cannon was Ganny's mother. She was a schoolteacher and later a school principal.*
- ♥ *Robert (Bob) was Ganny's husband. She calls him "Daddy" when talking to her children.*

Zachary and Anna had three children:

- ♥♥ *Mary (or May May or Ganny)*
- ♥ *James is only mentioned as playmate in early years.*
- ♥ *Saville is the brother who died at age one whom Ganny remembers by putting hyacinths on his grave.*

Ganny wrote her memoir for her five children. In order of their birth, they are:

- ♥ *Robert (Obbie), a salesman, married Mary Eleanor, and settled in Chattanooga, Tennessee. Two children, Bob and Mary Steele. Mary*

Eleanor ran a bookstore in her home ("Read More Books"). Obbie told the same story over and over every night at the dinner table about a rude little girl. We children were not pleased.

- ♥ *Saville (Bill or Billy) went to Vanderbilt. Married Renie and became a colonel in the Marine Corps and was stationed in Camp LeJeune, North Carolina. Later settled in Charlottesville, Virginia. Three children, Billy, Fay, and Ann. Uncle Bill wrote and self-published several handcrafted books of poems and stories. At the dinner table he told us stories about a dog "Siccamaclas" who belonged to the Old Witch. Though it too had a moral, we liked it better than Obbie's story about the rude little girl.*
- ♥ *Cannon went to Vanderbilt University and worked in the Office of Strategic Services (O.S.S.) while in the Army. A lifelong bachelor, he traveled all over the world and sent us gifts from exotic places. My favorites were Chinese pajamas, a View Master, and a set of Uncle Wiggly books. His career was a mystery, but it is likely that he worked for the C.I.A. Ganny kept hundreds of letters he wrote her, masterpieces about his travels and what he was reading, and what he was sending her to read.* [See Addendum for one of these letters.] *He died in at a young fifty-three in Ensenada, Mexico, and was buried in the Clark plot at the cemetery in Indianola, Mississippi.*
- ♥♥ *Lucile (Teeny), my mother, met my daddy, Billy Garrard, in New Orleans while she was at Newcomb and he was working for the Federal Compress. Two children, Mary and me. After a year in Shaw, Mississippi, they settled permanently in Indianola, where Daddy farmed cotton and soybeans and raised cattle.*
- ♥ *John married Bessie and worked for an oil company. They had two children, David and Gail. They lived in Jackson, Mississippi, Shreveport, Louisiana, and later Bartlesville, Oklahoma. When David and Gail were only eight and six, Bessie died of cancer. When we visited them in Jackson, John took us out every night for ice cream.*

Others mentioned: Aunt Laura was Anna's sister. She was married to Uncle Turner, a rascal who pops up in unexpected ways. Delle and Edie were Robert's sisters. Miss Lucie was Robert's mother. Tommy was Robert's younger brother. Ganny was born in Verona, in northeast Mississippi. She grew up in Nettleton and Okolona, and later lived in Tupelo. These were tight-knit communities, so it is no surprise that her family, the Trices, were at times in business with her future husband's family, the Clarks.

Chapter I

Ganny's Memoir

Sunday
June 5, 1956
Teeny. I'll get out the lap board, pen and paper and write yours. It will have to be just plain facts as I don't have much gift for writing—any talent you all have in that line you certainly inherited from Daddy. However, I want all of you to know that from your great-grandparents on down, you come from educated people—they went to college and sent their children to good colleges.

They were fortunate in that they were born between the Revolutionary War and Civil War, a prosperous time in the South.

About 1878 Papa sold out to Grandpa Clark at Verona. They paid him $50,.00 in cash, and he moved to Okolona. He and Mr. Zack Harper opened a big mercantile business there, "Trice and Harper." Uncle John Trice established the Okolona bank.

The town was growing at that time—the R.R. yards were there and it was the biggest and best town in N.E. Mississippi.

I remember the Round House full of engines and we had two passenger trains a day. One went North at 10.A.M. one South at 3.P.M. Quite an event and we always watched for them and waved.

On March 12th 1879, Papa and Mama married and went to New York and Niagara Falls on their wedding trip, then lived at The St. Elmo Hotel while the home was being built. I was born there Dec. 25th, 1879. The family physician was Dr. Miller who married

Mattie Harris, a niece of Grandpa Clark's. They were Erskine Miller's parents. Mama was always a bit leery of Dr. Miller. He was an agnostic and she feared his treatments would not prove effective on that account—but the only other doctor, old Dr. Green, was a confirmed Spiritualist, saw ghosts when he was called out at night, so Dr. Miller won.

We had a very beautiful home, more than 15 acres in the lot, then a ten-acre field across the road East of us where oats were grown. There was a large pool in the center with fish and we'd try to catch them with bent pins for hooks. It was a hundred yds from our front steps to the gate, a long brick walk, on each side was a row of cedars and arborvitae, then a row of water-oaks, then two very pretty "Summer-houses," they were latticed and covered with honey-suckle, then pear trees on the left and peach and apple on the right. We had fruit from May till the last of November.

The house was painted white, two bedrooms, the parlor, winter dining-room, latticed summer dining-room, a wide hall with a swinging lamp in the center, kitchen and large servants' room. The back porch was an El, and on the front porch were Wisteria and Akebia vines. I can smell them now, and the honey-suckle, also the Marshal Neil roses that grew in front of the bay window.

We had one of the few cisterns, most people had wells. The pump house was covered and next was a bath house with a big zinc tub, then the ice house filled with saw-dust where blocks of ice were kept all summer. Behind the back yard was another orchard of peaches, cherry, plum, Siberian crab apples and strawberry and raspberry vines. Then came the hen house, the "backy," the big barn and pasture. On the South side of the house was the flower garden enclosed with a paling fence which they hoped would keep the chickens out, but every day one or two old Plymouth Rock hens would get in and scratch.

It was a formal garden, the beds bordered with violets inside the pointed bricks. I remember roses—especially a Moss Rose—Hyacinths, Pansys, Johnny-Jump-Ups, Fushias, Geraniums, Lillies, and Ox-eyed Daisies.

South of us was the Murdock place and he raised fine cows, had a big Jersey bull that would come roaring right through the fence. We were scared to death of it. They finally put up barbed wire which was new at that time.

I think the first thing I remember clearly was walking to church, a good half-mile, Papa with a stove pipe hat and Mama with a bustle. She didn't believe in working horses on Sunday, so we had to walk. After dinner Papa would hitch Almont, a beautiful thorobred to a gig, take me for a ride, after which I'm sure he made for Mr. Milton Brown's race track which was about half-way to Grand Pa Trice's country home 8 miles east of Okolona.

When I was two years old Papa brought me those figurines I still have from New Orleans. When I was five he took me to Memphis and showed me a steamboat, the Rosalee. We stayed at the Gayoso Hotel. In a week or so after that he went to New York and brought me back a brown velvet dress $25.00 and Mama a black beaded seal-skin coat $50.00. This caused quite a sensation in the family. Every time anyone took a trip they borrowed the coat and I wore the dress made over and over time after time till I was in my teens. Then Mama made a silk quilt out of it. We got our money's worth.

In those days groceries were bought in large quantities and kept locked up, flour in barrels, meal and potatoes by the bushel. 50 cans of lard. vinegar and molasses in jugs. Coffee was green—it had to be parched, then ground and made in a tin coffee pot and settling with an egg shell.

There were no bakeries until about 1890. The Dahmers, a German family, came and opened one. Mama sent my brother for our first loaf—it was hot when they wrapped it up and he sat on the plank walk halfway home and ate it up, said it "smelled so good."

Everything was different then—even the clocks ticked slow and easy. Now they're in such a hurry.

My first sorrow came when I was five years old. Little Saville died in the fall, The following Easter I walked alone to the cemetery North of town, fully 2 miles, to put a bunch of hyacinths on his grave. It was cold and frosty! However, at Easter time our place was lovely, the Wisteria and Akebia vines in bloom, the fruit trees, and on each side of the front walk was a large Snow-ball bush. People would come a long way to see them. In the back yard, the two big mulberry trees would be hanging with green fruit 1½ inches long. When it was ripe we lived in the trees and ate with the birds.

In the fall great wagon loads of wood, hickory and ash and pine for the kindling would be brought out and a negro would be chopping and splitting it for days, big back-logs and smaller for the fire-places and stove-wood for the kitchen. All neatly piled. The chips were used too. We loved fires made with them.

About this time, maybe in June, Mama had a letter from Daddy's mother—we called her "Miss Lucie"—saying Delle would arrive on the 3 P.M. train, spend the night with us and go out to the Baker neighborhood next day. This was the first time I saw her and was told not to comment on her hand, but she talked about it and we were all astonished that she could do everything we did. She said the only thing she'd never been able to do was crochet. We thought she was so sweet. Uncle Johnny Baker came for her early next day, horse and buggy, eight miles to go and it would take at least 2 hrs. to make the trip. This was her summer vacation and the others envied her.

My brother and I were very happy, we had a Shetland pony, he had a Shepherd dog named Robin. I had a white kitten with a blue ribbon and we had a canary which sang all the time. When it died we buried it in the Summer House. I put flowers on the grave for a long time.

When I was six years old the family persuaded Mama to teach in a private school for girls only. Uncle John Trice bought desks and a black board and a school room was fitted up. They objected to the public school on account of boys. That's how Mama's teaching career started.

The first winter we had a big blizzard—snow and sleet stayed on the ground for several weeks. My brother and I made sleds out of kitchen chairs and could slide all over the place.

In a year or two Mama was elected to teach the Prymary class at the public school—so we all were enrolled there, but the boys and girls were not allowed near each other, didn't even use the same stairs to Chapel and boys sat on left, girls on right with a wide aisle between. The school house is there just as it was 70 years ago.

At that time the same custom prevailed in the churches, men on the right, women and children on the left. Then there was the "Amen Corner" where the old men sat and shouted "Amen!" during the sermon. In the big beautiful old church at Verona Grandpa Clark, Grandpa Cannon, Old Mr. Raymond, Uncle Bob Trice, Mr. Sam Long, and old man Bass composed this corner. None of them wanted Mr. Bass, but they couldn't keep him out. He was a miser, used white sugar himself and made his family use brown. They talked of ostracizing him.

Grandpa Trice lived in his big house eight miles east of Okolona, near Caldwell Lake and not far from the Baker neighborhood. The house was white, two story with columns. All the woodwork and staircase were solid walnut. Uncle Tom and Aunt Mollie Walton lived there too. They had ten children. Every summer Aunt Mollie would send the surrey for Corinne and Mary, my brother and me, and we'd spend a week in the country, which was a big event in our lives. I had never been anywhere but to Memphis and Verona.

Aunt Molly spent her time painting. I remember her landscapes, mostly snow scenes and covered with diamond dust. She was asked to exhibit her pictures at the Aberdeen Fair and planned to take Estelle and me down with her. My clothes were all packed when Mama heard Aunt Molly was going to raffle off one of her pictures. So I was not allowed to go. I never got over that blow.

In the fall, everybody old and young, went out to their place to gather scaley-barks, hickory nuts, chestnuts, black walnuts, and pecans.

The men would spend the night on the lake and fish—then next day there'd be a fish-fry. Frank Trice, one of the family darkies that we all loved, would cook the fish and pone corn bread and Aunt Molly took several freezers of ice cream and two or three cakes, chocolate layer, cocoanut and plain white "Lady Cake," light as a feather. When hog-killing time came she always put in for us and Uncle John's family back-bone, spare-ribs, sausage and even hams. She was a wonderful woman.

But when she was at her easel none of us dared enter the room. She kept a long buggy-whip by her side and would make a wide swoop and didn't care who she hit.

On these hickory-nut hunts we'd have to ford Tombigbee River at a place called Rocky Ford, near Camargo. Of course we'd be scared to death and excited and wonder if we'd ever reach the other side.

On late Saturday afternoons my Brother and I always sat on our gate- posts and watched the wagons, loaded down, going South. After a rain the bees-wax mud was deep and sticky and only oxen could pull a wagon. Men would walk along by them and most of the time they were drunk and staggered along, which we thought was very funny.

Okolona had plank walks all over town and the business section had brick walks, so we considered ourselves more progressive than Verona.

Once a year, in the summer we'd pack up and go to see Grand-pa Cannon and the other relatives. We always hoped old Herk Knowe would be on the train. He was a half-wit, rode up and down the M&O free and begged, but he wouldn't take anything but a nickle. If you offered him a quarter he'd shake his head and pass on. At Shannon there was an old water-mill and the big sight on the way up was to see the wheel turning in the water.

Grandpa's home was a beautiful, white house in a grove of oaks and like others in those days occupied a whole block. People raised everything to eat and the first man to display a radish in the spring was very proud. Aunt Maggie, Grand-pa's third wife, was still baking biscuits in a covered oven before the wood fire. The kitchen was some way from the house. Grand-pa was afraid of fire. His children didn't like Aunt Maggie—they thought people weren't nice unless they came from S. Carolina or Virginia, and she came from Alabama. She did look funny, always wore grey, looked like a pussy cat and wherever she went, day or night, carried an umbrella and a lantern.

Aunt Sally Bledsoe with Oscar and Cannon generally met us there. Florence and Mary Lou staying with Uncle Oscar.

Aunt Neppie had eight children and Aunt Mamie two, so there was quite a crowd of us. Uncle Will Turner had a small grocery store and would give us candy. I was always scared of Uncle Nat Hay.

We stayed two weeks to the day and after our visit some of them would come to see us and stay two weeks.

If any of my cousins came, the first night Papa would tell us to hang up our stockings. Santa Claus was coming. He always found something to fill them with but I don't know how. We never saw an orange, banana, English walnut or such things from one Xmas to another.

About this time Papa went on a church strike. The preachers were uneducated—preached sometimes 2 hrs and said nothing, so he said he was tired of their harangues and could get closer to his Maker out in the woods. This caused great consternation, but I was on his side and wished I could strike too.

Dr. Weir was the Supt. of Verona school at that time and also the minister at the Methodist Church, the only church there at Verona. He performed all the wedding ceremonies, baptized all the children, and buried all the dead in our families. Everybody loved him, but one Sunday he let a man play a violin in the church! Uncle Nat got up and left and never entered a church again.

I couldn't wait for Sunday to come when I was there because Grand-ma Clark always got happy and shouted. The back seat was reserved for the family darkies and when Grandma started up her cook would begin, one wild shriek after another. It was really something.

When I was about eleven years old the Frisco R.R. was started. When they tried to route through Verona the people were indignant and refused to sell them a right of way. So when Tupelo got the new R.R. it killed Verona. All the old families were swelled up about it and hated Tupelo. Gradually tho the younger members had to have jobs and landed at Tupelo. Uncle Bob Trice's boys, Mr. Raymond's, Mr. Kincannon's, Mr. Leroy Taylor's went into business up there and moved their families. All but Uncle Dave. He opened a drug store where T.K.E's is now but said he'd never live there, so he walked back and forth on the M & O four miles—every day. I don't suppose he would have walked on the Frisco.

Grandpa Clark moved his bank up there—it was on the corner of Main St. and the street parallel to M and O.R.R. Uncle Hugh Kincannon was cashier and ran it.

Way down in Okolona we heard of these things and of course the Memphis Appeal and the Avalanche carried much news about the Frisco R.R.

Papa was still making his yearly trip to New York. Once he brought back a roll of toilet paper from the Astor and showed it all over town. People had never heard of such a thing. After that everybody cut up patterns and all the tissue paper they could get hold of.

Then a Northern Co. put up a saw-mill at Nettleton and Uncle Turner built a big supply store there and announced he was going to move to Nettleton. Such a family upheaval as we did have! We thought Aunt Laura was going to quit him. She said there was nobody there but riff-raff and she was sure they would all die of malaria in that swamp. But Uncle Turner built her a big two-story house and she finally agreed to move.

Uncle Jim Trice built across the street and they moved in. He farmed the Caldwell Place which belonged to Grand-Pa Trice. My Papa was born in a log cabin on Caldwell Lake in 1849 while the big house was being built.

All at once things began to happen to us. Papa was offered a job as book-keeper for the big saw-mill and Mama was made Prin. of the new school at Nettleton. So our home was sold and we moved to Nettleton. It was a crude town, but I liked living there. Sweetgum trees everywhere. John Clark was at school in New York. Susie at I I & C and Richard very small, so Aunt Laura kept me with her much of the time. Uncle Turner had horses and I rode a lot. I was about 12 years old at this time.

Aunt Laura was always trying to make money as she said Uncle Turner was stingy and didn't think about anything but trying to leave a big estate when he died. She was always asking him where her $5.00 was that Grand-Pa Trice gave her when she married. He'd tell her he bought cattle with it and they all laid down and died. She'd get so mad she'd quit speaking to him.

Well. She planted ten acres in strawberries and shipped them. All of the children were rounded up at picking time and she paid us 1 ¢ a box. Daddy came over from Verona and stayed two weeks to make his Xmas money. So the first time I ever saw him was in a strawberry patch in June. I thought he was the cutest thing—so tall! Guess I made eyes at him all day, but he just picked and didn't pay me any mind.

The mill sawed up most of the pine in about three years, pulled up stakes and left Nettleton flat. So there was moving day again. Uncle Turner sold out to Mr. Bryant and moved to Tupelo. The Bank of Tupelo had been built on corner of Main and Spring and he and Uncle John Clark built the supply store where the old bank had been. Grand-ma Clark died about this time and Grand-pa just gave up business. They said he sat on his front porch and cried most of the time.

He went to Tennessee in the 1840s to buy mules. Met Susan Hodges, married her and she rode back to Miss behind him. She was only 13 years old. Her first child Elizabeth was born when she was only 14. Elizabeth was Cousin Molly Law's mother and died when she was born.

Dr. Weir was getting old so he retired and moved his family to Starkville. Prof. Street was elected principal of Verona school. He offered Mama a place as his assistant and we moved to Verona during the summer of 1894.

We were to live in Aunt Laura's home there but had to wait for Aunt Fanny Crawford to move back to the country. Uncle George Crawford had died and Grandma Baker and Aunt Fanny came to Verona to send the children to school. For about three months we lived in one of oldest houses there—put together with pegs instead of nails.

At this time Grand-pa Cannon became very ill—he was 86 yrs old. Aunt Sallie came over from Grenada to help nurse him and brought Oscar and Cannon with her. Aunt Mell was living at Sheffield and of course wanted to come. It had rained and rained and the roads were impassable almost. So Uncle Pink got a covered wagon with oxen and they came plodding into Verona one afternoon. Aunt Sally, Aunt Mamie, and Mama were embarrassed—they were so proud, but all of us children thought it was great fun, and we were dying to ride in that covered wagon. It took them two days to make that trip, not over 40 miles.

Grand-pa soon died and was buried in Columbus. Mama went down to see that he was buried by the side of her Mother. She always said he loved her mother more than any of his three wives. Grand-pa was the only person who called me Mary DuBose and I loved it.

Mississippi was now going through "Hard Times"—no jobs, cotton selling for 3 ¢ a pound. People lived out of their gardens and everybody of course had a cow and chickens. The only meat we had was salt pork and a little beef brought in from the country once a week. There were no canned vegetables and all winter we lived on bread and potatoes. At night we roasted sweet potatoes in the ashes.

Papa became very sick with what they called "Dropsy." I've seen Dr. Spencer insert a glass tube in his side and draw a foot-tub of water from him. This had to be done about every two weeks.

Verona was a deserted town. Mr. Alf. Raymond had killed his cousin - Mr. Alf Walker and skipped the country. Mr. John Armstrong had died on a fishing trip and Cousin Lilla took Lottie and went to Holly Springs to teach music in a girls' Seminary there. Earl and Ruby stayed in Verona with their Grand-ma Taylor. When the news of Mr. Armstrong's death was brought to Cousin Lilla she fainted in Mr. Will Raymond's arms. They later got married—he said he had always loved her.

The summer I was 16 Daddy and I were going everywhere together—and I was pretty sure I liked him best. Jimps Rogers was coming to see me every Sunday but his nose was too long. The

Verona boys just hated the Tupelo boys and when they came to see us would take the wheels off their buggies and all such things.

My first sweet-heart was Edgar Parchman, an Okolona boy. We were in the same grade at school and led our class. In the Spring he used to bring me shoe boxes full of Magnolia Frascati. When I'd go to visit Estelle Walton he'd rush me and he gave me a little diamond ring. I kept it hid.

The spring of 1896 I finished at the Verona school. Just after the War Papa left for college and took a business course at Trenton Tenn. Then came home, went to work and helped Grand-pa put all of his children through college. So Uncle John Trice wrote Papa he wanted to send me to Belmont with Corinne and Mary. All the girls in Verona envied me and Daddy packed his trunk and entered Draughn's Business College at Nashville. He'd come out to see me as often as they'd let him. Oscar was at Vanderbilt and I'd love seeing him occasionally. Then a man from Nettleton named Moman Morris that Aunt Laura wanted me to like was at Peabody—he was very good-looking but sort of pigeon-toed and he just worried me to death. He was fully 25 years old and I thought he was an old man.

This was the year of the Tennessee Centennial and Uncle John came from Tampa to see Corinne and me graduate, then stayed a week and took us to the fair every day. One day Corinne and Mary caught him flirting with some woman and so they cried and begged to go home. I bet they told Aunt Mamie. I wouldn't have tattled on my Papa for anything. While I was at Belmont Genie Morgan died and Aunt Molly sent me all of her clothes. They were made by Worth and fitted me exactly. I had the prettiest dresses of anybody there, but had to wear the brown and tan uniform when I went anywhere. We all hated our uniforms, but I realize now they were lovely.

Soon after I returned from college Aunt Sally and Cousin Mary Lou came to visit us and I went back to Shellmound with them.

It took two days to get there. We went from Verona to Tupelo, waited for the train to Holly Springs, changed there for Winona and from there to Greenwood where we spent the night. Oscar brought the surrey for us next day. Cousin DuBose Cannon was working for Uncle Oscar and I saw him for the first time. He was Mama's double-first cousin. Oscar and I had lots of fun that summer—he finished building the gin and I blew the first whistle. He was having a big time with two daughters of the Methodist preacher named Mr. Price—he called one "Hot Stuff" and the other "High Price." While I was there Daddy wrote me he was coming over and we'd get married, but finally Miss Lucie talked him out of it as we were both so young.

The following winter was the coldest I've ever known—chickens and cows froze in their tracks. Papa was still sick and had to sit wrapped in blankets before the fire in order to keep warm. Daddy came to see me one night and nearly froze walking back home—only two blocks—he said he slept between two feather-beds that night.

The following summer I had a few music pupils and in the fall Jimps Rogers got me a job as music teacher at the Oakland Normal Institute seven miles east of Fulton. He said he wanted to put me at the end of nowhere so nobody could find me. Uncle Nat Hay was travelling the country for Rogers Gro. Co. and he took me out there. I don't think we said one word the whole way.

The school was owned by the two Holley brothers—well educated men and they did a lot for the people way out there in Itawamba Co. Old Mr. Hall, Mrs. Andrew Holley's father, was a very wealthy man. Kept his money in a strong safe as there were no banks anywhere near. He sent Mr. Holley to Washington to see the Inauguration of Pres. McKinley and we thought he'd been to the end of the world.

I had a nice music class and in my spare time I learned book-keeping.

One day a man brought an old violin there to sell. I bought it for $5.00. It had "Stradivari and 1600–1700" inside. When I left there I had to leave my trunk and violin to be brought later. They failed to send the violin so I asked Uncle Nat to bring it on his next trip. He said "No. I'll not carry fiddles around for anybody."

Daddy wrote me he was coming for me at Xmas time and of course I <u>was pleased to death</u>. He had a double buggy with strong horses and looked very grand when he drove up late one afternoon—however he said it rained on him all the way, but wasn't very cold.

We decided to start at 4 o'c the next morning. It was smack dark and bitter cold and had stopped raining. This made the roads sticky. The farther we went the worse it got—the wheels would go down to the hubs in the mud. Daddy would clean out between the spokes with a fence rail—then we'd try it again. Finally the big iron pin in the double-tree broke and we were left sitting in the mud. He walked to a country store and bought six of these pins and some peppermint candy sticks.

We ate a little breakfast before we started and I heated some bricks and wrapped them in a blanket to keep our feet warm—of course they were soon cold and we nearly froze—didn't have a bite to eat but the peppermint candy till we got home at 10:30 that night. Our families were walking the floor! I don't remember how I went back to Oakland, but Daddy certainly didn't try it again. I forgot to say we only had one of those pins left when we at last drove in home. Time after time we were left sitting in the road.

The summer of 1899 Papa got so much worse we knew something would have to be done. The doctor was having to tap him every three days and he was growing weaker. Uncle John had been going to Indian Springs Ga. every summer and said that the water there was as beneficial as a spa in Germany where he'd been.

So Papa decided to try it and I went with him. We went to Tupelo to get the train for Atlanta and Dr. Elkin came to the station, took me aside and told me Papa couldn't live to get back home. He was always a gloomy-Gus and I didn't believe him.

When we got to Indian Springs the doctor there gave him three big doses of Epsom Salts 15 minutes apart. He could hardly swallow the last dose. Then he was told to drink all of the spring water he could hold. He began improving right away, never had any more dropsy and was a well man when we went home a month later. After that he went to Indian Springs nearly every summer.

The month I spent there was wonderful. We stayed at the Calumet owned by Mr. and Mrs. Elder. Rosa, their daughter, was my age and a darling girl. Their son Eugene was a Med. student and he was so attentive to Papa. I wore his diamond ring all the time I was there and if it hadn't been for Daddy I'm sure I'd have loved him. He wrote to me for a while after I left.

The big Hotel was The Wigwam and there were many smaller ones, all full, so the place was just swarming with people. I had a chance to do all the things I couldn't do at home—danced, played cards, everything. Papa looked on and enjoyed it all.

One afternoon Dr. Elder and I went to Flovilla, a nearby town, and I drank my first Coca Cola—it was much stronger than they are now and I felt so funny and didn't like it much. I think it had just been put on the market.

There was a man there from Macon Ga, very wealthy, about 30 years old. They said he owned nearly all of Macon. We went to a big picnic one day and he stayed by my side constantly, begged me to marry him then and there. I thought he was crazy—he was one of the flabby-fat kind and all his money and fine clothes didn't help him. Rosa and I called him "Old Sqush".

When Papa and I started for home we received a wire from Uncle John saying Aunt Mamie was to meet us at Atlanta. There she was at the station when we arrived and we learned she had heard of a famous fortune-teller there and she wanted me to go with her to see the woman.

She paid to have my fortune told first to see if the woman was any good.

It's hard to believe, but she never asked us a question. She looked at me a long time, then said, "You live west of here and are on your way home. When I think of your father I'm in great pain—he's been very sick. You've been with him at somewhere for a cure. While there you met a man you are almost in love with but there's one back home that you'll marry." Aunt Mamie must have believed in her for she had her fortune told but wouldn't let me hear it.

Shortly after we got home Papa was offered the job of bookkeeper for Trice-Raymond Hd'w Co. and Mama was offered a position as primary teacher in the Tupelo school. So we decided to move up there. Cousin Wilder had just built his big house and I was sent to call him over the phone from Uncle Joe Clark's livery stable, the only phone in Verona. It was my first time to use a telephone and I was scared to death. Could hardly tell him we wanted to move into the house they were renting as soon as they moved out.

Daddy didn't like this move at all. We had agreed to marry as soon as he was 21 and just before we moved he gave me my ring.

The Cumberland Telephone Co. had just put in a system at Tupelo. Mr. Mullen was manager and Ruby was day operator. She and Mr. Mullen soon fell in love so she quit and I got her job. I worked there till the day before I married. That's when I wore my feet out walking back and forth on gravel pavements four times a day. But I sure kept up with everything that was going on in Tupelo. Listened in on all the conversations and I heard plenty! However, I couldn't tell any of it so it wasn't much fun after all.

A week before we moved to Tupelo I went back to Okolona for the last time. I had a pale green organdie dress that Daddy was crazy about. Uncle Tom Walton had a shoe store and Bob [Bob must refer here to her fiancé.] gave me a pair of slippers to match my dress. I thought they were the prettiest shoes I ever saw—size 2 ½. Guess they couldn't sell them they were so small. That was the last time I saw Aunt Mollie as they moved to Oklahoma. I gave Edgar Parchman his ring and burned my bridges behind me.

There was a very pretty girl who had just moved to Verona named Madge Stanley, and Daddy went with her some. Of course I was awfully jealous and afraid to leave him down there with her, but he came to see me twice a week and things continued to go smoothly with us. The week before we married a crowd came up from Verona for a party at our house and during the night Mama heard Madge Stanley begging Daddy to marry her. She was terribly upset and wanted me to <u>do something</u>—what I don't know. I told her if Madge could get him she could have him. I never did tell anybody that George Lumpkin was begging me at the same time to run away and marry him. I wouldn't have had him if he'd been the last man in the world. He and Nanny Turner married a month after we did.

I never did like weddings—people all around you sobbing and taking on and I tried to get Daddy to slip off quietly somewhere and get married, but he wouldn't do it. So on the 21st of Oct. 1900 we were married in the house on N. Church St. at 6 P.M.

The parlor was not large and the crowd really closed in on us. Uncle Turner and Daddy's father were not speaking on account of the law-suit, so the two families lined up on opposite sides of the room, the men all slicked up in their broadcloth suits. Grandpa Trice and Grand-ma came up from Okolona and besides our families there were present Lottie, Ruby, Nelle Trice, Dr. Elkin, Mr. Mullen and Emmons Turner. Lottie played the wedding march and "Call Me Thine Own" during the ceremony. Just as it was over we heard a booming voice, "Hello! Tom," then "Hello! Brother

Turner" and the whole thing turned into a reconciliation party. They really stole the show. I threw my bouquet and Ruby caught it. Then Delle, Edie, Daddy and I made our getaway.

It was pouring rain and altho the side curtains on the surrey were up we got wet. And of all things, Daddy's new derby hat blew off and he had to find it.

We all finally got to Verona and dried out.

There were our gifts. Uncle John Trice $50.00, Corinne and Mary a silver carving set, Aunt Laura gave me a sewing machine, Uncle Turner a Jersey cow, Lottie and Ruby a picture, Dr. Elkin a little gold clock, Delle and Edie a silver soup tureen, Tommy a punch bowl with twelve cups, and Daddy's Mother and Father gave us a bedroom suite. Grand-ma Trice brought me a quilt which I loved. That night was the last time I ever saw her and Grand-pa as they moved to Oklahoma soon after and both died there.

Daddy and I lived with his family for about six months while our house was being built. Delle was teaching in Corinth and Grand-ma Baker was living in Verona at that time.

I had never known Edie before as she'd been at MSCW [Mississippi State College for Women] but that fall we were together all the time and I learned to love her very much. We spent most of our time doing "fancy-work." Then on Saturdays we helped at the store.

Daddy kept the books, his father bought cotton, and Mr. Seawright was the clerk. They were beginning to worry about collections—times were still hard, so they gave us a list of people who must not have anything charged to them. One Saturday I saw Edie writing something in the back of the day-book. She said she couldn't charge this person anything as he was on the list, so she was putting it where they wouldn't find it.

Uncle John Trice's bank at Okolona had been compelled to take so much land away from the people it made him very unpopular. So he pulled up stakes and moved to Tampa where he made a million in the Cigar and banking business. He kept Papa supplied with boxes of Cuesta-Ray cigars all his life. Papa always said anybody who smoked cigarettes or wore patent-leather, pointed-toed shoes was a "Sissy" and he had no use for him. Daddy did both and when he went to ask for me I told him not to smoke. I was so afraid Papa would say "No".

Miss Lucie kept a lovely home, Mary Liza—Chink's mother—cooked for her and she had trained a 15 yr. old boy named Morton to wait on the table. Kept white duck coats for him. He also helped with the flowers. Everybody had pits to keep them through the winter and in summer they were put on shelves on the porches. All colors of geraniums, Lemon Verbena. Fuchias and Rose Geraniums were the favorites. Grand-ma Baker had a Century Plant which had been in her family a long time. They bloom every 100 years and this one bloomed the year we were married. Aunt Cecile's prize package was a Lemon tree which bore constantly. She said she had never bought a lemon. Miss Lucie also had "cold-frames" and forced violets which she shipped to St. Louis twice a week. She had been shipping for years and saving the money to fix the house like she wanted it. She finally accumulated $2.00 and got her wish—put down hard-wood floors, added some to the house and furnished the parlor. It was lovely—the carpet was pale blue Axminster with wreathes of light pink roses—woodwork white with a little gold. One day we all went to Tupelo and when we returned found the parlor covered with black soot. The chimney sweeps had swarmed in the big chimney. It was an awful time! But we got rid of it by opening all the doors and windows and fanning it out with big palm leaf fans.

Grandma's room was just like her, furnished with her old mahogany and she kept pillow-shams on her bed, starched very stiff and trimmed with torchon lace. We could hear her clock ticking and striking all over the house.

Daddy's mother was so pretty, curly white hair parted in the middle and done in a knot on her neck. Lovely skin and her eyes were dark grey, almost black. She walked with her left shoulder a little lower than the right, a family characteristic. Every afternoon she had Morton crack a big tray of hickory nuts and scaly barks and we'd sit around it after supper and eat. She thought they were good for her. Of course Daddy was generally reading. We took Munsey Magazine and couldn't wait for it to come. At that time the two new books were Quo Vadis and When Knighthood Was In Flower. I had never read much, the Elsie books, Pansy books and Augusta Evans Wilson's were about all, so these new ones were very exciting.

All during the law-suit Daddy's mother and Aunt Laura had visited each other, they were congenial and loved each other very much. Aunt Nettie was never a favorite in the family. She'd go to sleep at night in your face. Of course I've been known to do that, but not because I was doped.

When Thanksgiving came Edie and I gave the dinner and we invited Mama and Aunt Laura. We swiped some of Grandma's black-berry wine she'd made for Sacrament and flavored the whipped cream—wondering all the time if they'd eat it. They certainly did—smacked and wanted more. Miss Lucie knew about it and winked at us—it tickled her.

I've always thought our marriage did a lot to reconcile the families. After the lawsuit was over and they began seeing each other again all agreed Mr. Walter Keys was largely responsible for all the trouble. He had married Grandpa Clark's youngest daughter Susie and boasted that he'd "married a barrel of money and was going to have it." Well, he failed to get it. Most of the estate went to Uncle John, Uncle Turner, and Uncle Bob Clark's heirs. The younger children got very little.

In December all of us got a sad blow. The plan had been for us to go to The World's Fair at Chicago the following Spring—it was to be our wedding trip. Well for some reason the fair was postponed for a year.

Soon after our marriage the little Cumberland Presbyterian Church at Verona was dedicated. Edith joined and I moved my membership. Grandma Baker built that church single-handed—ever since I could remember she'd been asking for contributions from everybody she knew and finally succeeded in getting enough to build it. She had more energy than any person I've ever known. Her maiden name was Nancy Word. Her mother was a Pittman and her grand-mother a Carrington and supposed to be of the English nobility. The family used the Carrington coat-of-arms on their stationery.

In 1849 Grandma married Robert Enos Baker—they lived in Monroe Co. at the "Baker neighborhood." When the war broke out Grand-pa Baker organized the 43rd Regiment of Volunteers—he was 1st Lt. He died in Aug. 1862 of camp fever in the home of Gov. Winston at Gainesville, Ala. Grand-ma was with him when he died and brought his body back to Monroe Co. in an ox wagon. He was buried in the Word Cemetery.

We liked to hear Grandma talk of her early life. How she taught her negroes to spin and weave, then dye the cloth with black walnut juice. After she came to Verona she was still making lye soap and knitting sox. Her closet shelf was crowded with her home remedies and she made poultices and doctored everybody around there. She told us that during the war there were no doctors to be had way out there in the country. She nursed and cared for many a sick person. One of her slaves, a young girl, was unable to give birth to her baby. Grandma worked with her for two days. Then when she saw she was going to die, made an instrument out of a steel barrel hoop and delivered the child. It died, but she saved the girl's life.

She had lots of trouble through the years—lost her property after the war and then Uncle Will, her youngest son shot and killed a man in Aberdeen. How they saved his skin I don't know, money and influence maybe.

After Daddy's Mother died Grand-ma lived with Uncle Will and Aunt Janie. She had worked for years on the family tree—then when she was very old got mad with it one day and burnt the whole thing up.

The fall we married Daddy was very busy—had to work lots of nights on the books. I'd go to the store with him altho it was so dark I could hardly get there—no lights at all. I think I just stumbled around the whole time I lived there, but of course I didn't complain as Verona was very jealous of Tupelo's electric lights. I was scared to death half the time too.

Soon after Xmas our house was started and we watched every brick, every plank and every nail and when it was finished I thought it was the prettiest house in the world.

We moved in about the middle of March 1901. Daddy's Mother told me she didn't know how she was going to get along without me after having me there. I thought she was sweet to say that and I never forgot it, but I'm afraid I said nothing as I'm always tongue-tied and dumb at the wrong time.

Tommy wanted to stay with us all the time—he was about 11 yrs. old. They'd have to come for him every night. They had a time with Grandma too. She picked supper time to do her visiting and somebody had to go out and hunt her up every night.

Our place was large and Daddy started a garden right away and a water melon patch and we had lots of flowers. Ours was the first moon vine seen around there. We saw it in a catalog. It was on the front porch and covered with blooms. Traveling men would see it from the train and go in the store to ask Daddy about it, which pleased him.

Old Josh worked for us and Delia did our washing.

The summer of 1904 Daddy's mother got sick—they said it was "Bright's Disease." She died Oct. 4th 1904.

Every summer during her life she had invited Miss Belle to stay there during vacation. She was teaching at MSCW. Well, in the spring of 1905 Papa announced he and Miss Belle were to be married. Delle and Edie refused to stay there unless he built an upper floor to the house—which he did.

Daddy never wanted to live in Verona after his mother died, so we sold our home to Mr. Tom Milam and moved to Tupelo the fall of 1905.

Now I've told you everything I can remember and all my secrets. The rest you know.

It may be hard for you to wade through all this, but I've had fun thinking over old times.

It seems like I've lived such a long time—there have been so many changes. When I die I don't want anybody to grieve for me—just remember I was always so happy.

Mother

Chapter 2

Signs and Silences

In March of 2022, the coronavirus pandemic was wreaking havoc on all our lives, and we were reeling from the attack at the U.S. Capitol on January 6, 2020. At the time that these events were traumatizing both country and world, my daughter was diagnosed with breast cancer, and my son was going through a divorce. I struggled to find a way to help. In the middle of these crises, I had a dream that woke me up. It was early morning, in the darkest hour before dawn. Though the dream was only a fragment, the electric currents going up my spine said it was important. It was about Ganny:

> *I am on a trip with Ganny. Maybe a treatment for her? Immersion in water. I make sure she's all right.*

I got out of bed and groped my way down the hall to the living room and turned on the light. The hinged door to the secretary creaked when I opened it. I took out Ganny's memoirs. The dream had led me to them. Having raised five children, she would surely have answers for me.

• • •

I had read her memoirs several times in my youth, but this time was different. This time her words came alive.

Her memoirs begin with her birth in Okolona, Mississippi, in 1879, and end just after her marriage. On previous readings, I regarded her words as a complete story, an endearing story, a sacred text that I dared not analyze or challenge. This time I was angry. Why had she stopped at her marriage? Why had she withheld the very things I most wanted—*needed*—to know? About the births of her children. What it was like to raise them. Most urgently, why had she said nothing about my mother? And next to nothing about her own mother?

Within her parameters, she told the things she wanted to tell. Though she told them beautifully, she left out one thing: her feelings.

I had to remind myself again and again that she didn't write her memoir for me. As she declares in her first sentence, she wrote it for her five children. She had a right to write what she wanted and how she wanted. Who was I to protest? But I protested. Thankfully, the crises that led me to the memoir were ultimately resolved, but my issues with Ganny had only begun.

• • •

She was "Muddy" to her children, "May May" to her relatives and close friends, and "Ganny" to me and her other eight grandchildren.

She wrote the date—June 5, 1956—at the top of the first page of her memoir, but until now, I hadn't thought much about it. This time, when I stopped to do the math, it hit me. She wrote her memoirs when she was seventy-seven. *Exactly my age*. Double sevens, a favorable sign. Sacred numbers.

She recorded her observations by hand in an ordinary black three-ring binder on seventy-six 5 × 8-inch unlined pages. She made copies by hand for each of her five children, all nearly identical, though in comparing my mother's to her brother Billy's copy, I saw a few minor differences. Among other things, the salutations are

White – Two bed-rooms – the "parlor"
winter dining room – latticed summer
dining-room – a wide hall with
a swinging lamp in the center –
Kitchen & large servants' room – The
back porch was an El – and on the
front porch were Wisteria & Akebia
vines – I can smell them now –
and the honey-suckle – also the
Marshal Neil roses that grew in
front of the bay window –
We had one of the few cisterns –
most people had wells – The
pump-house was covered & next
was a bath house with a big
zinc tub – then the ice house
filled with saw-dust where
blocks of ice were kept all summer –

Handwritten page from *Ganny's Memoir*

different, Mother's copy begins, "Teeny, I'll get out the lapboard, pen & paper & write yours"; his begins, "Billy, you asked for this, so I have my pen, paper and lap-board and will see what I can do about it." Other differences suggest that she wasn't just recopying, but in places she modified her story according to which child she was writing for. Another amazing thing: to my knowledge, she didn't write any preliminary drafts, which means that she must have spent time composing her thoughts in her head long before she wrote them down.

On this reading, I was appalled by the first sentence: "It will have to be just plain facts as I don't have much gift for writing." *Why? Why does it have to be plain facts?*

I tried to understand. She may have wanted to set herself apart from other memoirists who romanticized, sentimentalized, or trivialized their lives (and their feelings). She'd grown up in the Victorian era, a time when girls were brought up to be ladies, charming and *silent*. She'd written the memoir in the 1950s, a time when our culture was in full-fledged denial about family dysfunctions. Reasonable speculations, but they didn't satisfy me. I wanted more.

In the rest of the first sentence, she says ". . . as I don't have much gift for writing." This assertion dismayed me, for it is blatantly untrue. On its terms, the memoir is a masterpiece constructed with a sure hand. She limited the scope and defined her time frame, birth to marriage, and chose a reportorial style by which to tell it. Much as I might protest these limits, they served her and her purpose.

Her voice rings true. She sounds like nobody but herself. A light tone. An eye for the quirky and unusual. As one who taught writing and literature for over twenty-five years, I can say with confidence and absolutely no bias that she has a distinctive flair and an easy, flowing style. "Everything was different then," she says, "even the clocks ticked slow and easy. Now they're in such a hurry."

Her detailed descriptions are as convincing as Jane Austen's. Her tone is as light and humorous as Lawrence Sterne's. And in her fondness for the "em" dash she's in the company of Emily Dickinson. The people she describes are as vivid as any Dickens character. We can see Old Man Bass, the miser who eats white sugar while his family eats brown. We can hear the rascally Uncle Turner telling his wife the tall tale that he bought cows with her $5.00 dowry, but they all died. We see him, stalking out of a Sunday service, enraged at the irreverent fiddler who dared to play his instrument in a church. And then there's poor, disgraced *doped* Aunt Nettie, falling asleep at the dinner table.

• • •

Some omissions are justifiable because her children already knew them, though some things would bear repeating. The feud, for instance, that is only alluded to between the Clarks and Trices that culminated at Ganny's wedding. Why omit this delicious drama? Was it too embarrassing? Was she protecting someone? And who was Walter Keys? The one who bragged that he got a barrel of money when he married Susie Clark. I wanted more! And what about Uncle Will? Ganny only tells us that he shot and killed a man in Aberdeen. Why? Why did he do it? Did he get away with it? And Mr. Alf Raymond? Why, in heaven's name, did he kill his own cousin?

Startling as they were, these questions are minor. I wanted to know more about Ganny. What she was like on the inside. What forces shaped her. What held her back. What moments expanded her. Diminished her. Yet, maddeningly, at every opportunity for self-disclosure, she feints.

Though we lived in the same house for twenty-one years, I cannot say I knew her.

I had to remind myself again and again that she didn't write her memoirs for me. She wrote them for her children, her audience of five. If the audience shapes the story, and it does, her audience of five shaped hers, shaped what she said—and what she didn't say. I had to conclude that Ganny gave them the version of herself she thought they wanted and left out the rest.

If I wanted more, there was only one thing to do. Sleuth. I would look for her in the space between the words. I would look for moments when she unintentionally gives herself away.

I began to see that even in keeping the distance between herself and the culture she's describing, something was communicated. When she's trying hardest for an impersonal, reportorial style, her tone at times gives her away. In noting the rivalry between the town folk of Verona, Okolona, Nettleton, and Tupelo, that in other hands might seem petty, her light tone conveys her affection. "All the old [Verona] families were swelled up and hated Tupelo," she says. Though she doesn't state it outright, her animated tone shows she's on the side of progress when she learns about new inventions—the roll of toilet paper her father brings home from the Astor Hotel, her first Coca Cola, her first call on the telephone.

At the beginning of her memoir when it might be natural to introduce her family, she describes their home instead, the landscape, flowers, plants, and shrubs. On and on she goes in minute detail: The house was set on a lot of "more than 15 acres" with a long brick walk and "a row of cedars and arborvitae—then a row of water-oaks—then two very pretty 'summerhouses'—latticed and covered with honey-suckle—then pear trees on the left and peach and apple on the right—we had fruit from May till last of Nov."

When she finally mentions living beings, it's the old Plymouth Rock hens that broke through the fence and the big Jersey bull that scared her to death. When she finally gets around to her parents, she says only that they walked to church on Sundays because Mama "didn't believe in working horses on Sunday." After giving this tiny glimpse of her family, she gets back to the facts, saying that her parents, Zachary Taylor Trice and Anna Maria Cannon, were married in 1879, the year Ganny was born. Momentarily, I wondered if . . . but no. They were married in *March* of 1979, and Ganny was born on Christmas day, *more* than nine months after her parents were married. Whew! (From what I later learned, Anna would never have had a child out of wedlock.) Instead of telling us how her parents met or how they got along, she tells us they went to New York City and Niagara Falls on their wedding trip and lived in a hotel in Okolona, Mississippi, until their house was built.

She tells exactly one story about her mother. In choosing a doctor for the delivery of her first child (who was Ganny), Anna had to decide between the family physician, Dr. Miller, an agnostic, and Dr. Green, a "confirmed spiritualist" who saw ghosts. Ultimately, she decides on Dr. Miller, the agnostic. It is an amusing story, but it tells me nothing about my great-grandmother or what it means that she chose the agnostic. Was she more afraid of the man who saw ghosts than the one with no opinion about God?

I looked again at Ganny's *first* memory, that they had to walk to church because her mother didn't believe in working horses on Sunday. In her second mention of her mother a few years on, Ganny says she was all set for a week-long visit to Grandpa Trice's house outside of Verona that was "a big event in our lives." Yet when Anna finds out that Ganny plans to go to the Aberdeen Fair where there's to be a raffle (!) she won't let her daughter go. Ganny says, "I never got over that blow." Given how few times she expresses her feelings, it seemed to be a clue that Anna was overly strict and that Ganny resented it. Later evidence would prove me right.

I found out more about Anna in a self-published book by Mother's brother Saville. She was born in 1854 and died in 1943 at the age of 89, placing her squarely in the middle of the Victorian era in England and the Gilded Age in America.

It was a time when girls were trained to be ladies, selfless and self-effacing. A lady put others first at the expense of her own needs. Her talents, such as singing or playing the piano, were for the pleasure of others, never for herself. A lady was to be useful: she was expected to learn to sew or quilt and make poultices for the sick.

Men were brought up to participate in the public sphere, while ladies were to manage the home and the children. Boys and girls attended separate schools or separate classrooms and, as Ganny notes, took different stairways to chapel. At church, men and women were separated, men sat on one side of the aisle, women on the other.

A poem written in 1862 by Englishman Coventry Patmore, wildly popular in Anna's day, is about the ideal qualities he looked for in his wife. She was to be selfless in her devotion to her children and submissive to her husband. One stanza goes:

> Man must be pleased; but him to please
> Is woman's pleasure, down the gulf
> Of his condoled necessities
> She casts her best, she flings herself.

The poem's influence was enormous and created a culture (or cult) that idealized women as "Angels in the House." In *Professions for Women,* Virginia Woolf notes a variety of these unrealistic expectations: An angel "must charm . . . sympathize . . . flatter . . . conciliate . . . be extremely sensitive to the needs and moods and wishes of others before her own." She must "excel in the difficult arts of family life."

Ironically, women themselves sometimes upheld these values more stringently than men. Anna was probably one of them.

I learned in another book written by my uncle Saville, *A History of Northeast Mississippi,* that Anna began teaching in a private school for girls *only because the family begged her to.* "Beg" is a strong verb, and I wondered if it was chosen to justify the taboo back then against a married woman who worked. I also wondered if, despite the family's cover story of "begging," she might have had an unacknowledged ambition because a year or two later, she was "elected" to teach in the public school and later became principal of the school in Nettleton.

And why did these schools want her? Apparently, they liked her sense of propriety. In a "Tribute to Mrs. Anna Trice," celebrating her twenty years' service to the city schools, a woman named Sara Frances Mitchell says, "Teaching was to her a sacred privilege and in every little child she saw possibilities of strength of character and purity of soul." [See Addendum A.]

But how did this propriety play out in her role as a mother? Made her excessively strict, I concluded. After all, she kept Ganny from going to the fair because of a raffle. "I never got over that blow." Strong words for a reticent memoirist. It isn't far-fetched to believe that Anna would also have taught her daughter to stifle her emotions and suppress her naturally buoyant spirit.

In contrast, when talking about her father, Ganny is more open, and her partiality to him is evident. When he decides to go on a "church strike," she wishes she could strike too! When she goes on a trip with a married uncle and his daughters to the 1897 Tennessee Centennial and his daughters see him flirting with other women and cry to go home (to tell their mother), Ganny says, "I wouldn't have tattled on my Papa for anything."

Ganny's affection for her father was mutual. Zachary dotes on his only daughter. He brings her gifts from his travels that she treasures. After a trip to New Orleans in 1881 he brings her two China figurines, romanticized figures of a boy and a girl. Ganny kept them all her life and passed them on to me. When her father brings her a brown velvet dress that costs twenty-five dollars, she wears it for years.

If Anna stifles her, Zachary wants to expand her world. On a trip to Memphis when she is five, he shows her the steamboat "The Rosalee," and they stay at a fine hotel, The Gayoso. When Ganny attends Belmont College in Tennessee, Zachary packs his trunk and enters Draughn's Business College in Nashville to be near her. "He'd come to see me as often as they'd let him," she says.

Though Ganny never directly describes her feelings about her father, she captures him in descriptive details: She says he smokes cigars and declares that any man who smokes cigarettes or wears patent leather shoes is a sissy. Every night after dinner, Zachary hitches his "thoro-bred" horse to his gig and takes Ganny for a ride. After the ride, she suspects he goes to "Mr. Milton Brown's race track," but she doesn't seem to disapprove and probably wishes to go with him.

If uncharacteristically expansive about her father, Ganny slips into vagueness about her two brothers, and at first I couldn't understand why. She says that her first sorrow was the death of her brother, Saville, when she was five and that the following Easter, she walked two miles to put hyacinths on his grave. This trek would have been a challenge for most five-year-olds, and scary, but she doesn't mention her fear and says nothing about her grief. (Maybe in this instance, she doesn't have to. Her actions say it all.) Then she abruptly changes the subject to the weather ("cold and frosty").

She says that she and her brother were "very happy"—playing with their pets, sitting on a gate post to watch people passing by, and sitting high up in the trees eating Mulberry fruit with the birds. But these activities aren't those of a boy of four. Puzzled I pulled out the bottom drawer or the secretary, dug through it, and found a genealogy showing that, in fact, Ganny had two brothers. The older one was James Madison Trice, whom she doesn't mention again after her brief description. The younger one, Saville, was born in 1885 and died the following summer. It was his grave she visited. Understandable that her suppressed grief over his death made her writing oblique.

Chapter 3

Her Legacy

After I'd gleaned what I could from Ganny's silences and wondered where to go next, I had another dream. Not really a dream, only an image—but it woke me up:

> *Ganny and I are mulching and fertilizing a tree outside her bedroom window.*

The tree, an oak, was vivid. We were hard at work. The dream seemed to be saying *keep going*. It seemed to say that, together, Ganny and I are fertilizing the *family* tree.

◆ ◆ ◆

Since Ganny never mentions her forebears, I began to think they must have been charlatans or outcasts. But then I discovered "Genealogy of the Trice Family from the Seventeenth Century" Cannon retrieved from a source he didn't identify, and according to the date on the postage stamp, he sent it to Ganny in 1954. It meant that she had it in her possession before she wrote her memoir yet doesn't mention it. I wonder what she'd think if she knew it can now be found on the internet.[1]

On Anna's mother's side, according to Cannon's letter, Albert Beatrice, who lived three centuries before Ganny, was a Scotsman who fell in love with Mary Dunbar, *a maid in the court of Queen Elizabeth the first.* According to the account, he wants to marry her and emigrate to America. But Mary is so charming that the queen can't bear to let her leave the court and forbids her to marry. But when Mary sobs, cries, and begs without ceasing, the queen relents and lets her go. Once freed, Mary marries Albert.

Upon immigrating to America, like so many others, Albert and his brother shortened their name from Beatrice to Trice, believing it would be more palatable on the tongue of their future countrymen. Too bad. Beatrice, on any tongue is more musical than Trice and is an allusion to Dante's beloved Beatrice, inspiration for *The Divine Comedy.* Not only did Albert lose a beautiful name but by changing it he lost all claims to any Scottish inheritance.

According to another document, this one without a verifiable source, Ganny's mother, Anna Maria Cannon Trice, was a descendant on her father's side of Rasha Cannon, who was himself a descendant of Herman Melville, the author of *Moby-Dick!* Herman Melville was a descendent of Thomas Melville, who was one of the Sons of Liberty in the Boston Tea Party.

The basic story line is validated by a genealogical sketch of the family tree made by Jim Trice, Ganny's nephew. In his sketch, Anna Cannon's line can be traced back to Edward III, king of England from 1312–1377. Another forebear was a close companion to Henry VIII. There's even a Plantagenet in Anna's history.

Why did Ganny never mention her amazing ancestors? Maybe she didn't put much stock in genealogy or doubted the source. More likely, she preferred to think of herself as just plain folk.

Chapter 4

She Blooms

Without a word about her adolescence, Ganny skips from childhood to early adulthood. She was one of the few women in her time and place to attend college, Belmont College for Women, in Nashville, Tennessee, yet she mentions this accomplishment only in passing.

Among my discoveries, I found Ganny's diploma, rolled up and lying in the seemingly bottomless bottom drawer all this time. It has an embossed seal with a blue ribbon attached. *Belmont College* is written in fancy script at the top of the diploma. The date of her graduation on May 26, 1897, is at the bottom. Beneath that are signatures of the Regent and two principals on one side and the faculty on the other. In a small, fine script are the Latin words *Aliquid Excelcius.* My sister and a friend of hers, both Latin scholars, translated this inscription to mean "somewhat higher" or "somewhat excellent." Oh dear. Trifling words to celebrate a remarkable accomplishment, a college education rarely achieved by women of the time. As if to add insult to injury, Ganny is identified by her diminutive nickname, "May May."

If Belmont College's attitude toward a woman's education was ambivalent, so was the culture, and so was Ganny. Though she skips over her own accomplishment, on page one of her memoir, she says in her third sentence, "I want all of you to know that from your great-grand-parents on down—you came from educated people—they went to college and sent their children to good colleges." From other letters, I learned that her mother, Anna, and her grandmother, Mary Suzanne DuBose, both went to Darlington Academy in Darlington, South Carolina.

For a while, I stewed over Ganny's belittling diploma. I finally realized that the two women schoolteachers who founded Belmont in 1890 may have been playing it smart. They knew that their best chance in founding a woman's college at that time was to be humble about it. *Aliquid Excelcius.*

Ganny gave me advice only once, and it was about my education. When I was in tenth grade and in the throes of making an agonizing decision as to whether to go to boarding school, I found a handwritten note from her on my pillow: "I want you to have a good education so that you won't ever have to feel inferior." Endearing, until I saw the mixed message. She wanted me to get an education only so I wouldn't feel "less than"?

But life gives her what Belmont hasn't—confidence, independence, and a sense of accomplishment. In the fall after graduation, she reports that "Jimps Rogers got me a job as a music teacher at the Oakland Normal Institute" near Fulton. Though she doesn't say it directly, of course, I sense her excitement and have the proof when she uncharacteristically buys herself a gift, a violin. The inscription inside says "Stradivari 1600–1700." When she pays five dollars for it, she doesn't know, can't know, it's the trade of a lifetime but also priceless. It's her *real* diploma, a rightful commendation for completing her courses, for her mastery of music, and most of all, for her love of music.

Tragically, the violin is lost when she moves to Fulton. Uncle Nat Turner, who agreed to help her move, leaves the violin behind, saying, "No, I'll not carry fiddles around for anybody." (Remember him? The one who had a thing against violins and walked out of church because of a musician playing his violin in church.) As to how Ganny *felt* about losing the violin, she doesn't say.

Flash forward to 1954. Ganny saw an advertisement in the *Commercial Appeal* by a man from Fulton, Mississippi, asking $1500 for a Stradivari violin, and she wondered if it is hers. She *wondered?* How many Stradivari violins could there have been in Fulton, Mississippi? There's more. On May 12, 2022, I saw an article in the *New York Times*, about a Stradivari violin that was auctioned by a person named Toscha Seidel for twenty million dollars. And as if that wasn't enough, shortly after I that, I ran across a poem called "God Needs Antonio" by George Eliot. Here's the last verse: "'Tis God gives skill, / But not without men's hands: he could not make / Antonio Stradivari's violins / Without Antonio."

In 1899, two years after she graduated, Ganny's father became extremely ill. He'd suffered for years with what the family doctor, Dr. Elkin, diagnosed as dropsy. It's called edema today and linked to congestive heart failure (a hereditary disease and the primary cause of my mother's death at sixty-eight). According to Ganny's account, when Zachary's condition worsens, a cousin advises him to go to Indian Springs, Georgia, for a "water cure." Ganny goes with him.

Before they leave, Dr. Elkin warns Ganny that her father "probably couldn't live to get home." But Ganny is undeterred. She says that Dr. Elkin has always been a "gloomy gus" and that she doesn't believe him.

The name Indian Springs is a nod to the Native Americans who first learned of the healing properties of spring water. It works for Zachary. After a regimen that requires local spring water and regular doses of epsom salt, he recovers. Though Ganny doesn't say it outright, a new exuberance in her tone suggests that the trip is life changing. She says, ". . . the place was just swimming with people. I had a chance to do all the things I couldn't do at home—danced, played cards, everything." For the first time, she feels the freedom and independence she hasn't known at home; for the first time, she is taking care of her father instead of the other way around; for the first time, she is free from the restrictions of home—and Mother.

For the first and only time, Ganny bubbles over with *feelings* as she embraces each new experience. Her style becomes looser, more expressive, at times downright chatty. In the nearby town of Flovilla, she tastes her first Coke, just on the market. "It was much stronger than they are now," she says, "and I felt so funny and didn't like it much." What she probably didn't know is that "coca" refers to cocaine, and the original formula called for small amounts of it, legal at the time.

She and her father stay at the Calumet Hotel, and she gets to know the owners, Mr. and Mrs. Elder. She makes friends with the Elders' daughter, Rosa. Even though she has a sweetheart back home (Robert Clark) dying to marry her, she writes that she's crazy about the Elders' son, Eugene, the medical student taking care of her father. She confesses that she wears Eugene's diamond ring all the while she's in Indian Springs (apparently forgetting that she's writing to her children). She says, "If it hadn't been for [Robert] I'm sure I'd have loved him." She adds that though she's sought after by several other suitors, she is only interested in Eugene.

What?

• • •

While pondering the change Ganny undergoes while at Indian Springs, I remember my dream, the one that started it all. The one that got me out of bed to seek Ganny's memoir. This one:

I am on a trip with Ganny. Maybe a treatment for her? Immersion in water. I make sure she's all right.

Now it made sense. *I am on a trip with Ganny.* As is the way with dreams, things are mixed up. Instead of Ganny going on a trip with her father, I am going on a trip with her. A psychological trip. *Maybe a treatment for her?* The treatment for her father becomes *my (psychological) treatment of her.* My new understanding of what she says in the memoir, what she doesn't say, and what it means. The attention I am giving it is becoming a treatment for *me. Immersion in water.* Baptism. New life. Since characters in a dream are always first and foremost about the dreamer, it means new life for me. A literal allusion to the healing waters of Indian Springs for Ganny's father *and* the healing Ganny receives from her new, expansive expression of feelings *and* the healing that was taking place in me.

Released from constrictions of being a "lady" or "angel," Ganny spontaneously expresses herself, her inner self, her authentic self. In confiding her crush on Eugene, she is *not trying to please anybody but herself.* She forgets she is writing for her five children who might not want to know about her mad crush on a man other than their father. She is "full" of herself—in a good way. *I make sure she's all right.* At this point in her life, even if it doesn't last, she is fully herself. Fully all right. In writing about her, I'm seeing that the Ganny in me is all right too. I'm seeing her *rightly.*

Chapter 5

Her Marriage and Beyond

After Ganny's year of teaching music, the Trices move to Tupelo. Ganny has taken on new responsibilities within the family and is designated to make the first phone call on the new and only phone in Verona to find out about a house for rent. She's fascinated that this telephone has been invented, but this is her first time to use one, and she is "scared to death."

Significantly, after reporting that Zachary is taking a job as bookkeeper for Trice-Raymond Hardware, she says, "So *we* decided to move up there." No longer a child in the family, she's an adult helping make decisions. Anna goes to work as a teacher at a primary school and Ganny as a switchboard operator of Cumberland Telephone Company. After eagerly looking forward to listening in on all the gossip, she says, "I heard plenty. However I couldn't tell any of it so it wasn't much fun after all."

When Robert hears that the Trices are moving to Tupelo (4½ miles away), he's afraid he'll lose Ganny and pressures her to marry him right away. But his mother intervenes and asks him to wait until they are twenty-one. (They were born in the same year.)

What does Ganny say about this man, my grandfather, Robert Baker Clark? Very little. Only that they met in her Aunt Laura's ten-acre strawberry patch where the young people were picking strawberries for a penny a box. She says she likes Robert's looks and "makes eyes" at him all day but that he doesn't pay her any attention. (Later, she learns that he planned to marry her the minute he saw her.) Then she admits a feeling. When he arrives to pick her up in Fulton at Christmas, she is "pleased to death" to see him. She tells only one story prior to their marriage about a harrowing buggy ride home in the rain. When the buggy gets stuck, one of the pins holding the wheel falls off—several times.

After they turn twenty-one, Ganny agrees to marry Robert but tries to persuade him to elope. She says she never did like weddings with "people all around you sobbing and taking on." (No surprise there.) But Robert insists on a church wedding.

She mentions him only once more. When he prepares to ask her father for her hand in marriage, she gives him tips on how to win over her father. Knowing Zachary's prejudice against men who smoke cigarettes or wear patent leather shoes, and that Robert does both, she advises Robert not to smoke in her father's presence but doesn't mention his shoes. Zachary gives his approval anyway.

In describing her wedding day on October 21, 1900, Ganny casts herself in a supporting role. She says nothing about her gown, her bouquet, or the church. Instead, she cryptically refers to a longstanding feud between the Clarks and the Trices—no lead-up, only the denouement. She says, "Uncle Turner and Daddy's father were not speaking on account of the law-suit so the two families lined up on opposite sides of the room—the men all slicked up in their broadcloth suits." After enigmatically mentioning the fortune hunter who caused the rift, she skips to the scene of reconciliation when Uncle Turner cries out in a booming voice, "Hello, Tom" to Robert's father, and Grandpa Clark responds with "Hello, Brother Turner." [See Addendum B for more about the rascally Uncle Turner.]

A popular ending for comedies and romances is, of course, the wedding. But in a post-modern way that I love, Ganny doesn't stop there but instead gives us a glimpse of her married life in Verona, her old hometown. Until their own house is built, she and Robert live with his parents; what might have been a difficult in-law situation is not because Ganny is fond of her mother-in-law, Miss Lucie, and vice versa.

Ganny describes family evenings after supper when they sit around eating scaly barks and read. Until her marriage, Ganny has read only children's stories such as "The Elsie Books" or an occasional novel by Augusta Jane Evans Wilson. Now she eagerly awaits the latest issue of *Munsey Magazine* and reads books she considers worthwhile such as *Quo Vadis* and *When Knighthood Was in Flower*. In these last pages, her preference for books over weddings is clear.

At night she goes down to the store to help Robert with the books. She's scared as she walks in the dark alone and wishes for streetlights but doesn't complain because "Verona was very jealous of Tupelo's electric lights."

When the new house is ready, after predictably describing the vegetable garden, the flowers, and a moon vine that catches the attention of travelers, she speaks of her fondness for Robert's mother, Miss Lucie. Before she leaves for the new house, Miss Lucie tells her she doesn't know how she will get along without her. And then Ganny says: "I thought she was sweet to say that and I never forgot it, but I'm afraid I said nothing as I'm always tongue-tied and dumb at the wrong time."

Her self-awareness surprised me.

Chapter 6

Gandaddy Clark

Who was this man, Robert Baker Clark, who so inconsiderately died just before I was born? I was told that he was a banker and that during the Depression he stopped a run on the Tupelo bank by holding a gun on anyone who tried to withdraw his money. Despite his patent leather shoes, he must have been just what Zachary wanted for a son-in-law—a manly man.

I found out from some clippings in the drawer that Robert grew up in Verona and lived in Tupelo for most of his adult life. He started out as a bookkeeper for his father's mercantile business before he became a banker. He was made president of the Federal Landbank of Tupelo and later president of the Federal Landbank in New Orleans. His election was noted in *The Times-Picayune.*[1] An article from the *Hattiesburg American* describes him in glowing terms:

> Although a citizen of North Mississippi, Mr. Clark is known throughout the entire commonwealth for his sound leadership and constructive service in behalf of Mississippi progress. His eminence as a financier elevated him to the presidency of the State Banking Association.[2]

The writer mentions other civic leadership roles including the state Y.M.C.A. and Hi-Y clubs.

Beneath these clippings, I found three letters from Gandaddy to Ganny before their marriage. I had never seen them. He addresses her as "May May" and signs them "Rob." As I read them, I remembered a photograph of them: he is at least a foot taller than Ganny and towers over her, looking like the stern patriarch. In these letters, he treats her variously as a little girl, an angel in the house, and a lady.

The first letter is addressed to her in Itawamba County from him in Verona. It is written on stationery from the family hardware store, "Clark Brothers: Dealers in Dry Goods, Groceries, Hardware, Boots and Shoes." It is dated "Friday, November 12, 1897," the year she received her diploma from Belmont and started teaching music. It was written three years before their marriage. It begins, "My dear sweetheart."

Ganny has apparently sent him a photograph of herself, and he says he was glad to see her "come out of that envelope and how I do wish it had been in reality!" He says the picture looks good but that he doesn't think she looks well and his mother, Miss Lucie, agrees. He chides Ganny for working too hard, as a full-time music teacher and teaching music pupils after her classes:

> Say, May May I do not like in the least the way they are doing you. I thought you were going out there to teach music and possibly spend some little time in the school but to make you a regular teacher and then have your music pupils outside of that I didn't think that was in the bargain and besides, little girl, you can't do everything.

He adds that he hopes she won't be "worried" with him if at times he says too much.

He says that on their last visit, she was cross from the stress of teaching and that "I will be awful glad to see you even if you are a 'cross old thing' and I know you can't be cross around me. I just won't allow it May May." (Before I became apoplectic, I had to remind myself that he was only eighteen when he wrote these letters.)

The second letter, also from Verona and addressed to her in Tupelo, is dated January 1898. It begins "Dear Little Girl." She has apparently asked him if he minds if she writes to a male friend, and he responds:

> No, May-May. Of course I don't mind your writing to Murrell, but it makes me mad when he walks up and says, 'Well I've gotten a letter from your girl today' and grinning from ear to ear.

So, he *did* mind. He describes the pain of being apart, declares his love, and says that nothing, except God, should ever come between them.

The third letter is written on October 3, 1898, on "Clark Bros" stationery and addressed to her in Grenada, Mississippi, where she was visiting her cousin, Oscar Bledsoe (who later introduced my mother to my father). Robert chastises her, saying that "it does look as if every time you go anywhere you get where there is some one sick but it is not good for you." He continues,

> How long are you going to be in Grenada, what is Mr. Bledsoe doing there anyway? Why is he not at home? You will be tired and broken down before you get where you can rest in peace.

He complains about the difficulties of their lengthy separation:

> I have received enough frustration already to do me a lifetime. Let me tell you little sweetheart this whole winter <u>shall</u> <u>not</u> pass without my accomplishing the thing I have already tried

> and failed to do, this little separation has made me more determined than ever we shall certainly marry before this winter is gone.

The letters he wrote when he was young were hard to swallow. But a telegram from him to her thirty-four years later indicates he may have mellowed. He was in Washington, D.C., on business and addressed the telegram to her at their home, 6 Dunleith Court, in New Orleans. The occasion is their thirty-first anniversary, October 21, 1931. He says: "Remembering the day and I love you thirty one times more than ever. RBC."

After Gandaddy's retirement, he and Ganny moved to New Orleans, and then to Jackson, Mississippi. I don't know the reason for either of these moves. When they moved to Jackson, they lived in The Edwards Hotel (later called "The King Edward"). Letters from other family members indicate that their children and grandchildren visited them there often. My sister remembers her visits and that they took her to dinner at a nearby restaurant. It was the Mayflower, a seafood restaurant that opened in 1935 and is still in existence. The original owners were George Kountouris and John Gouras, who had immigrated from Patmos in the Aegean.

How often does a person meet someone who knew her grandparents three quarters of a century earlier? When my husband Claiborne and I first moved to Jackson, we regularly dined at the Mayflower. One night, I told Mr. Kountouris that my grandparents used to frequent his restaurant while they were living at the Edwards Hotel in the 1940s. He said that he too once lived at The Edwards in the 1940s and asked who they were. "Robert and Mary Clark," I said, my heart leaping. "Did you know them?"

"Vedy well, vedy well!" he said, grinning broadly.

◆ ◆ ◆

The only other things I know about my grandfather I found out through letters written after he died. In the letter dated January 17, 1945, Daddy writes to Mother:

> There's nothing I can say to let you know how I feel because you know how close I felt to him. He was one of the closest friends I ever had or ever will have and in some ways I felt closer to him than my own father. I have always believed in an after-life and I'm sure we shall some day see him again.

Despite these discoveries, I have many questions about my grandfather Clark. Since Ganny didn't have my mother's difficult traits of moodiness, depression, and alcoholism that showed up in at least two of their children, I must wonder if these traits came from him.

I learned from my first cousin Gail Clark Held that her father, John, my mother's younger brother, was alcoholic. "He was charming, brilliant, and funny," she said, "except when he was drinking. Alcohol destroyed his character." In that phone call, I learned that her brother David, my beloved cousin, was also alcoholic, again making me wonder if the gene came from Gandaddy.

Because he was the patriarch, the independence Ganny experienced at Indian Springs seems to have ended at her marriage. She became an "angel in the house" who never made trouble, never expressed her feelings or needs.

Chapter 7

Angel in the House

Ganny ends her memoir by saying: "Now I've told you everything I can remember and all my secrets. The rest you know—" *Not true.* Despite how beautifully she describes people and places, she has left out how she *felt* about the important things.

That's the next-to-last sentence. It's the last one that gets me:

"When I die I don't want anybody to grieve for me—just remember I was always so happy."

I don't want anybody to grieve for me. These words were meant to comfort Obbie, Bill, Cannon, Teeny, and John, and maybe they did. But this time, on reading them, they made me cry because I heard the subtext: "Don't worry about me because I don't matter."

". . . just remember I was always so happy."

What did that Hemingway character say? *Isn't it pretty to think so?* On this reading, I was stunned by this phrase. It is not true. Not true for her. Not true for anybody. Ganny, like the rest of us, had her share of happiness, joy, sorrow, and pain.

For one who carefully contained her feelings from childhood on, one who didn't like weddings because of all the sobbing, why this ending?

To make her children happy. The buoyant spirit, the *joie de vivre* she expressed in Indian Springs, went underground to make others happy. It was what she was trained to do.

She was the angel in the house employing the ultimate soul-killing self-negating stoicism and selflessness. An angel who never fell from grace. She not only sidestepped her feelings in the memoir but evaded them in her life. I know because I was there.

Part II

My Memoir

Chapter 8

An Idyllic Childhood

After a time of thinking about my strong reaction to Ganny's memoir, I gained an insight: Telling the hard, dark parts wasn't hers to do. It was mine.

Carl Jung believed that every human being has a unique story to tell and that if one should fail to live it and tell it, he would become lost, alienated, or go out of his mind. Since I didn't want to become lost, alienated, or go out of my mind, I mustered my courage and began.

• • •

I was born in Greenwood, Mississippi, on March 5, 1945, and grew up in nearby Indianola. I was named Marion Moseley Garrard, all three names from the Garrard side. My arrival was at the worst possible time. World War II was raging and would not officially end until six months later, on September 2, 1945. Two of Mother's brothers were serving in volatile places, Cannon with the Army in Persia, Saville, a Marine, in Saipan en route to Japan when the bomb was dropped on Pearl Harbor. Daddy's brother Jimmy had been lost in action two years before. His brother Bobby was serving in the Navy, and his sister Mary Jayne had enlisted in the WAAC.

Two months before I was born, Gandaddy died, and Ganny came to live with Mother, Daddy, and Mary shortly thereafter. Ganny died when I was a junior in college, so in all of my growing up years she was there.

My maternal grandmother, Mary Dubose Trice ("Ganny"), as a young woman at Belmont College 1897

My maternal grandfather, Robert Baker Clark ("Gandaddy"), as a young man 1897

My sister, Mary DuBose Garrard, at age eight with me, Marion Moseley Garrard, at 8 months

In a letter from Daddy in New York on January 17, 1945, he says:

> Dearest Teeny,
>
> Was terribly sorry to get the wire about your Daddy just when we were all beginning to have hopes. There is nothing I can say to let you know how I feel because you know how close I felt to him.
>
> I do hope your mother is taking it all right and I want to renew my invitation for her to live with us.

The family of three would soon become a family of four and then five. Mother was thirty-five when I was born, considered late to be having a baby. If I could've gotten here sooner, I would have.

When I arrived, my sister Mary was seven years and seven months old. Family members on both sides recognized her precociousness. Daddy's brother Jimmy wrote from overseas about "Mary's self-acquired education," saying, "I don't know how to address her–as a child wonder, or to wonder if my spelling will be criticized." Cannon wrote to her when she was six and enclosed a sample of Persian numerals for her to decipher. In a letter from Cannon to Daddy when Mary was eight, he asked if he was helping Mary with her trigonometry and said he wished he could be a fly on the wall in her classroom. With the blessings of her teachers, she skipped the first grade.

The house we lived in on Sunflower Avenue was a white frame bungalow on the corner of a tree-lined street. It had three bedrooms and two baths, a one-car garage in back, a screened-in porch in front, and a breezeway on the side banked by hydrangeas with sky-blue blossoms.

In my first memory, I am two. I am standing on the back steps. They are warm to my bare feet. I have just had a bath. I am dressed in a sunsuit that ties behind the neck. My bare back tickles as beads of water evaporate. I am eating a salty cracker. Everything is satisfactory. I want nothing. My people are nearby, but the moment is mine.

Mary and I shared a bedroom. Ganny's was next to ours.

My nighttime Ganny was a felt presence. She welcomed me to her bed any time I woke up early or had a bad dream. I'd climb up, and she'd make room for me. Maybe she'd scratch my back or recite a poem:

> In the nighttime, at the right time,
> So it's understood, 'Tis the habit,
> Of Sir Rabbit
> To dance out in the wood.

By day, I would look into her twinkly blue eyes, and she'd wink at me. Everything about her was soft—her hair, her rounded belly, her dresses of cotton or silk. Photographs of her a young woman show her wearing her naturally curly blonde hair upswept like a Gibson girl, but by the time I arrived, it was fluffy and snowy white. She was small and sprightly. She was warm, gentle, and kind. She was unpretentious, always her very own self. Somewhere there's a photograph of her peeping at me around the shrubbery dressed in our Sunday best. She called me "Sugar" or sometimes, oddly, "Sugar Dump."

She placed herself at the perimeter of our lives, making sure she wasn't in the way, making sure she didn't upstage Mother, making sure she was useful.

Since we had a cook, Ganny made the extras, teacakes, gingerbread with lemon sauce, and fudge. I can still see the dark chocolate fudge on a pale blue platter—earth and sky. Her special treat was oyster stew. She had simple remedies for our childhood aches and pains, milk toast for stomachaches, and Campho-phenique for everything else.

She was often at the "machine" sewing while I played with scraps of material at her feet. I found a letter in which she describes making a sport shirt for her grandson David when he was five months old because his baby clothes "didn't look right on him." She made clothes for all my dolls and beautiful costumes of satin or taffeta for my dance recitals. When she made a quilt to send to her son Cannon, she included a note saying that "Marion helped with the backing." She was generous to call it helping. I don't remember the quilt or the backing or much that she sewed, but I do remember the comforting whir that came from her machine.

◆ ◆ ◆

Though Ganny's presence was comforting, my deepest bond was with my mother. I adored her. In my eyes, she was perfect. Always attentive and wise. On a vacation at the beach, when I fussed about sand in my bathing suit, she replied, "If you like the beach, you have to put up with the sand." A philosophy to live by.

I escaped polio, rampant at the time, but had measles, mumps, and chicken pox back-to-back. What luck! I had Mother all to myself to read to me. To her everlasting credit, she read me all fourteen *Oz* books by Frank L. Baum.

I wanted to be with my mother all the time. I'd wait for her outside her bathroom door when she took a shower. One morning while waiting, I climbed on a stool and began playing with her things, her perfume bottles, a jewelry case, and a china tray that held her bobby pins. My elbow must have hit the little pin tray. It went crashing to the floor, and the pieces scattered in all directions. Mother rushed out, saw the damage, and cried, "Oh, no! You've broken it. I loved that little tray more than anything in the world."

I looked at her, I raised myself to my full height of three feet, and said, "I would've-a thought you loved me more." At that she laughed and pulled me to her for a hug. She told me that story many times.

When she and Daddy went out to parties, though I was happy to be left at home with Ganny, I wanted Mother there too and longed for her to come home. One night I must have pestered Ganny one too many times about when they were coming. She dragged a couple of lawn chairs over to the curb where we could watch the cars go by and made a game out of who would see Mother and Daddy first.

Next to Mother, I loved my playmates and our neighborhood, a child's paradise. There was Barbara, a year older, across the big street, Sunflower Avenue; Henry, exactly my age, across the smaller street, Heathman; nine Hartness girls only two blocks away on Moody Street: Kay, Mary Ann, Gail, Louise, Lucy, Amy, Judy, Beth, and Barbara. (They had one boy whom I only vaguely remember.) The middle three girls were near my age, so if Mary Ann couldn't come over, I'd ask for Gail; if she couldn't come, I'd ask for Louise. Some days all three would come. A bonanza.

I was fascinated by the Hartness girls. They envied me because I only had to share my bedroom with my one sister. I envied their large and lively household. Mrs. Hartness seemed eternally *planted* at her sewing machine, the centerpiece of their living room. She sewed clothes for all the girls, beautiful clothes. I have a newspaper clipping of the girls gathered around Mrs. Hartness sitting at her sewing machine. The girls are in their Easter clothes. Except for their straw hats, they wear outfits their mother made, all identical: gingham skirts and boxy tops with four buttons and a wide collar.

My playmates and I had plenty to do right in my own backyard, our hangout. I had a swing set, a playhouse, and a sandbox. We chased each other barefoot in the grass, stopping only to pull stickers from the soles of our feet. We turned cartwheels and hung upside down on the monkey bars till we were dizzy. We made an unused brick barbeque pit into a queen's throne. In downpours, the street drains clogged up and made a pool two feet deep for us to splash in. We played dress-up, choosing outfits from a box Mother kept of old clothes, flowery hats, and high-heeled shoes. If we became bored with my yard, we'd go next door to Henry's and climb the live oak, its trunk entwined with a thick wisteria vine just right for footholds.

Playing was learning, and learning was play. I remember the moment when I realized that words could have more than one meaning. Ganny had invited three ladies over to play bridge. I tickled myself by greeting the first to arrive, saying, "Mrs. Early, you are early."

A natural teacher from the start, Mary taught me to read well before I went to kindergarten. She propped up a blackboard on our screened porch, wrote out the letters of the alphabet, and taught me their sounds. She also played the ukulele and taught me all of Mother's old songs and more. On the backseat with her while on a car trip, she tried to teach me how to harmonize. She taught me the melody and had me practice it. But every time she joined in with the harmony, I would sing harmony. Over and over, she tried to get me to stay on the melody—to no avail. I was (and am) the little sister who always followed her lead.

Mary would let me tag along with her and her friends to the swimming pool or the soda fountain. After she got her license, Mother let her take me places. Once, when she and her friends were going to take me to a birthday party, she realized she forgot to ask where it was. One of her friends who'd come along was sure she knew the way and directed Mary to a house out in the country. It was a birthday party but not the one I was invited to. In the long wait before we unscrambled the mix-up and Mary returned, I could only stare at their unfamiliar faces as they stared back at mine.

◆ ◆ ◆

Reading lesson with Mary

Home-schooling with Mary ended when I went to Mrs. Davis's kindergarten or her relaxed version of one. The only thing we did on a schedule was practice our reading at the three child-sized tables on her front porch. In the very first week, thanks to Mary, I was placed at the Bluebird table (for good readers), instead of the Redbird table (for pretty good readers), or the Yellowbird table (for slow readers). Did they think we didn't know what these colors meant?

At playtime, we girls twirled around in long skirts while the boys played with toy cars. At recess we'd take hoes to Mrs. Davis's garden and chop off the heads of garter snakes. As much fun as these activities were, my most vivid memory is the day that Henry and I ran away from kindergarten. As soon as he whispered his plan to me, we took off the minute Mrs. Davis turned her back. A couple of blocks later, we discovered a playground. Thrilled to have it all to ourselves, we ran from seesaw to swings to monkey bars to sandbox and back again. We discovered some reddish fruit we later learned were persimmons and ate our fill.

We'd only been missing less than an hour when the family Oldsmobile came into view. Mother and Daddy got out, walked unhurriedly across the playground, gathered us up, and ushered us back to kindergarten. Knowing we couldn't have gone far and that we were perfectly safe in our quiet little town, they weren't worried. Their composure about our disappearance took some of the fun out of it.

Chapter 9

Garrard Forebears

Only later did I notice my father. Before I go on, I'll tell a little about his people.

I had help in tracing my paternal line—a book called *Governor Garrard of Kentucky: His Descendants and Relatives* by Anna Russell des Cognets.[1] It is bound in leather, and the title is embossed in gold. According to the author, the first known Garrard ancestor was "a French Huguenot who left France [for England] soon after the Revocation of the Edict of Nantes, most probably about 1685." Des Cognets says she could not find any records of him and his two sons, but she describes many of their descendants, including my direct forebears:

- William Garrard and his wife Elizabeth settled in Stafford County, Virgínia, probably between 1730–1740.
- Their son, James Garrard, born in 1749, was "a staunch supporter of the bill to establish universal religious liberty" and the second governor of Kentucky. He and his family settled in Bourbon County at their home, "Mount Lebanon."
- James's son, Captain William Mountjoy Garrard I (1771–1838), was married to Susan Dalrymple Peers. He is the first of five William Mountjoy Garrards (the fifth and last was my father). He served in the Kentucky Legislature for many years. During the War of 1812, he became "captain of a troop of volunteer

state dragoons."[2] His austere portrait hangs over the mantle in my living room.

- ♥ Captain Garrard's son, Dr. William Mountjoy Garrard II (1818–1892) practiced medicine and law. He was married to Matilda Ann Coburn.
- ♥ Dr. Garrard's son, William Mountjoy Garrard III (1850–1881), married Zilpah Barrett. A newspaperman in Lawrenceville, Illinois, he died young, but left one son.
- ♥ The newspaperman's son was William Mountjoy Garrard IV (1881–1958), a "posthumous baby." He and his widowed mother moved to Greenwood, Mississippi, to be near her brother. He married Mabelle Moseley Smith, bought a home, "Rosemary," on the Tallahatchie River, and became an entrepreneur who founded a cooperative cotton association.
- ♥♥ The entrepreneur's son, William Mountjoy Garrard V (1909–1981), my father. He married Mary Lucile Clark of Tupelo and made a living farming.

Whew! I am glad I was born a girl. If I'd been William Mountjoy Garrard VI, it would be a weighty legacy to bear.

I don't know very much about my paternal grandmother, Mabelle Moseley Smith. She spent years tracing her genealogy and donated her findings to the town library in Indianola. She never told anybody exactly how old she was; even her marker on her grave says *Circa* 1882. (Granddaddy was born in 1881, so I suspect she was older.) Their children, in order of their birth, were:

- ♥♥ William (Billy), my father. He and mother lived briefly in Shaw, Mississippi, then Indianola. They met in New Orleans when she was attending Newcomb College of Tulane University, and he was working at the Federal Compress. Ganny's cousin, Oscar Bledsoe, introduced them. Two children, Mary and me.

- James (Jimmy). Married Ethel Keesler. They had two children, Charlotte and Mimi, and lived in Greenwood. Before joining the Army, Jimmy and Daddy were partners in farming cotton. Jimmy served as a tail gunner in World War II and was lost in action in the Mediterranean in 1943.
- Zilpha. Born October 16, 1911, and died on September 16, 1913.
- Mabelle. Married Buck White, a professional golfer, who played on the PGA Tour and won three times between 1946–1951. One child, Garrard. Mabelle and Garrard stayed at the guest house at Rosemary when not accompanying Buck on the golf circuit. When Buck retired, they moved to Hollywood, Florida. After Buck's death, Mabelle lived in Gulfport, Mississippi.
- Mary Jayne. Married Bill Whittington, a lawyer. They lived in Greenwood. Three children, Jamie, Billy, and Anna. Mary Jayne and Mabelle collected and edited *Allegiance*, a collection of Jimmy Garrard's letters from overseas during World War II.
- Robert (Bobby). Married Naomi who was from somewhere in California. No children. Bobby served in the Navy in World War II. He died in an automobile accident in 1951. After his death, Naomi moved back to California.

My paternal grandparents, William Mountjoy Garrard IV and Mabelle Smith Garrard, lived in Greenwood, Mississippi, in a spacious English Tudor house of stucco and timber. It was bordered by Grand Boulevard to the west and the Tallahatchie River to the north. The house, which they named "Rosemary" (for remembrance), was more cosmopolitan than southern—no columns, no front porch, no mint juleps. (They didn't drink.)

Chapter 10

At Rosemary

Every Thursday, my parents drove to Greenwood thirty miles away for a midday dinner to see my grandparents and other family members. Before I started school and in summers, I went with them. Rosemary was the setting for every holiday. At Christmas, Grandmother bought a tree as tall as the fourteen-foot ceilings. At Easter, she hid eggs (or had them hidden) under her roses.

I wish I could remember specific visits, but I can present a collage. Let's say I am ten. It is just before noon on a summer day. Arriving at the gates to my grandparents' property, my mother, father, Mary, possibly Ganny, and I pass through the stone pillars, circle around the guest house where Mabelle and Garrard stay when Buck is on tour, around a lily pond and a goldfish pond, and park under the porté cochere. I hear an eerie screech and soon peacocks emerge from the trees and strut across the wide lawn like they own it.

We park in the breezeway and enter through a screened door. Dressed as always in a crisp white shirt and debonair bow tie, Granddaddy meets us. Teasingly, he shakes my hand like I'm a grownup and ushers me in. I like him because he is soft-spoken and gentle. He has soft brown dancing eyes. Once inside, my eyes are drawn to the white marble lion in its place over the mantel of a large fireplace, its fearsome mouth open in a roar. It represents the lion on the family crest that Grandmother had duplicated on

Mabelle Smith Garrard,
my paternal grandmother

William Montjoy Garrard IV,
my paternal grandfather

Mabelle and Will's children in the garden at Rosemary: Billy, Mary Jayne, Jimmy, and Mabelle (Bobby not shown)

Mabelle and Will's grandchildren at Rosemary for Christmas: Charlotte, Garrard, Jamie, Mimi, Mary, and me

gold rings for her five children and my mother hand-stitched in needlepoint.

Mary disappears up the stairs, probably to join our older cousins, Mimi and Charlotte. I linger with the grownups. Grandmother sits in her usual place in the corner by the window, her crutches propped on the wall behind her. Mabelle slouches in a chair by the sofa in casual slacks and shirt. She is talking. Grandmother, hard of hearing, asks her to speak up. She depends on an unpredictable hearing aid pinned to her shirtdress.

Mary Jayne dashes in, fashionably dressed, her three children in tow. She hustles them upstairs and asks what she's missed. Mabelle laughs, begins her story again. Perhaps it is about a golfer Buck has run into at the Greenwood country club. She will pause for everyone to place this man and his people. They look at Grandmother who knows him and his complete history. This story, or maybe another one, reminds Mary Jayne of a story. She's told it before, but no one minds because it's the way she tells it that matters. Daddy makes only a quip, saving his best stories for his buddies at Weber's Truck Stop. Mother says, "Oh, Billy." Laura calls us to dinner.

The grown-ups eat in a formal dining room and now that I can sit still, I'm finally allowed to join them instead of eating at a small table in a nook near the kitchen. The fare is pheasant, quail, or duck that Granddaddy has hunted in nearby fields. The cooks, Laura and Magnolia, are unruffled despite the elaborate meal they have prepared while keeping the young ones quiet. Now that I am at the big table, I notice how expertly Granddaddy carves and serves the game and how patient he is when people ask for seconds before he's had a chance to eat.

Garrard, age fourteen, comes in late. He is followed by Laura, who sets his plate in front of him, his usual, a hamburger. I am jealous and want one too. Though I like the menu of game with all the trimmings, his hamburger is the height of sophistication. No. Garrard is the height of sophistication, knowing what he wants and how to get it.

After we eat, Jamie, Billy, and I go into the vast drawing room with paneled walls and a secret door that can only be opened if you know where to find the tiny spring to release it. We open it and shut it many times while we think up a good spy story. We go upstairs, past the gun room, past the door to the balcony, to the ballroom with its highly polished floors. We "ski" on them on our sock feet until our mothers call us to go home.

◆ ◆ ◆

My paternal grandmother was born in Benton, Mississippi. She spent years tracking down her Smith forebears and quipped to a fellow genealogist that it was a curse to be born with a name like Smith!

Mary Jayne describes her mother in her 2003 memoir, *Reveille*:

> My mother's patriotism was legendary. She knew by name every family member who had fought under the American flag since the Revolution. Long before President Kennedy was born she was asking not what her country could do for her, but what she could do for it.[1]

One summer, Grandmother challenged her eight grandchildren to learn the names of the U.S. Presidents *in order* and offered a five-dollar reward. For reasons I haven't figured out, I was the only grandchild who took her up on it. The next time we went to Greenwood, I proudly reported to Grandmother that I'd done it—memorized the presidents *in order*. "That's fine," she said and brought out a crisp five-dollar bill. I put it in my pocket . . . and waited. She gave me a nod that meant *Now go play*. Deflated, unable to guess that she intended it as a sign of trust, I walked away. But I can still say them: *Washington, Adams, Jefferson, Madison, Monroe, Adams. . . .*

In 1959, Mabelle and Grandmother were in a terrible car accident. Mabelle, who was driving, escaped with minor injuries, but Grandmother broke her hip, and they were both badly shaken. After the accident, Grandmother didn't walk again without her crutches, and although I'm sure she never blamed Mabelle, she never drove again.

◆ ◆ ◆

Granddaddy did not follow in the footsteps of his father, the journalist (although the writing gene showed up in Jimmy, Mabelle, and Mary Jayne); he became instead a businessman, a highly successful one. After receiving a degree in textiles in 1904 from Mississippi

State, he began working for Humphrey Cotton Company. He married my grandmother Mabelle Moseley Smith in 1908, and they lived in Indianola, where he acquired several thousand acres of fertile Delta farmland, envisioning a time when his sons would farm it.

In 1921, after his outstanding management of Humphrey Cotton Company, the directors of the newly formed Staple Cotton (now Staplcotn) in Greenwood recruited Granddaddy to become their general manager. One of the originators and Granddaddy's future partner was Oscar Bledsoe—Ganny's cousin. Granddaddy was primary representative and liaison to mills in New England, the Carolinas, Europe, and Japan. After he died in 1958, according to a National Cotton Council newsletter, while Granddaddy was at the helm, Staple Cotton sold more than ten million bales of cotton, valued at 1.5 billion dollars.[2]

The writer of the newspaper went on to say, "Mr. Garrard was known for his winning personality, courage, depth of character and unusual trading abilities." After Granddaddy's death, his successor, Dr. C. R. Sayre, described him as "a giant of a man who stood five feet four. He was handsome, dapper, self-assured—and surprisingly grateful for the least attention paid him, the smallest compliment given him."[3] The editor of a Delta Council publication said, "Under the leadership of Will Garrard, the Association earned an international reputation, and is today recognized as the largest and most successful cotton marketing agency of its kind in the world."[4]

Businessman that he was, Granddaddy deeply valued the arts and instilled their importance in his children and grandchildren. Believing that travel itself was a cultural education, he sent his three oldest grandchildren, Charlotte, Mimi, and Mary, to Europe in the summer of 1957. In a postcard to my parents, Charlotte indicated how important the trip was to them. "Simply having the most wonderful time I've ever had in my life," she writes. "Paris is out of this world. Decided to stay over another year so will see you next summer."

The trip was formative for all three. Charlotte would one day be the owner of Rosemary and all it entailed. Mimi would become a dancer and have her own dance troupe in New York. Mary would become an eminent art historian.

◆ ◆ ◆

Mary Jayne and Bill founded the Greenwood Little Theatre and supported the arts all over Mississippi. Mary Jayne founded the annual Greenwood Literary Seminar and invited prominent writers to speak, including Eudora Welty, Willie Morris, and Cleanth Brooks. My cousin Catherine Tomsyck told this story: At a luncheon Mary Jayne hosted in Eudora Welty's honor, Miss Welty became distracted from the conversation at her table by the talk at the one adjacent. Whipping around in her chair, she exclaimed, "Are y'all talking about Prince Charles? Tell me what you're saying. I just *love* Prince Charles."

In *Reveille*, Mary Jayne describes her three and a half years in the service in World War II. She begins with the moment Congress passed the bill in 1942 authorizing a Women's Army Auxiliary Corps (WAAC—later WAC). Jimmy and Bobby had both joined the armed forces, Jimmy in the Army Airforce and Bobby in the Navy, shortly after the attack at Pearl Harbor. Determined to keep up with her brothers, Mary Jayne joined the WAAC. She became a second lieutenant and was stationed in Victorville Army Airfield in the Mojave Desert in California and other places in the West and Midwest. By the end of the war, she'd been promoted to captain.

Although she admits that times in the service were often boring, routine, and dreary, she found the people she met endlessly fascinating and the women incredibly brave. She confides that she fell in love with a dashing lieutenant whom her family talked her out of marrying. A highlight for her was a special guest performer at the Officers' Club, Skitch Henderson. She says:

> Until Skitch Henderson was sent to B-29 training for overseas assignment, he occupied the piano bench at the club every evening before dinner. The junior grade officers rallied around to listen to Skitch's inimitable style and waited for one of his halts, when he would say, "This is Hank—or Doc or Ken." He would then improvise something that sounded exactly like that person. Amazing.[5]

Back at home after the war, Mary Jayne wrote a column "From the Delta," for a notable regional magazine, *The Delta Review*. In the opening paragraph, she writes in her inimitable style, about two women who revitalized the Indian Bayou in Indianola:

> Indian Bayou's banks are becoming the bonniest braes since Annie Laurie jilted her Scot and left him to doon and dee, in three-quarter time, at Maxwelton. This is no story of instant triumph for the ladies of Indianola, Mississippi, but a long, long tale awinding through 35 years of effort, frustration, and patience.[6]

Always more interested in Buck's career, Mabelle kept her urge to write a secret. A few years after she died, I discovered a stack of short stories in our storage room that she wrote while at Vassar College. In her nomadic life with Buck, it wasn't unusual for her to stash her belongings in various family storerooms, but for a long time they languished in ours because she'd stuffed them in a rusting bread box. I loved the stories, loved their Dorothy Parker-ish sophistication, irony, and wit. Regrettably, she never got around to writing about Buck's legendary golf career (though her son and grandson would later write about it). But fortunately, Mary Jayne extracted one piece from her for *The Delta Review* called "Par for the 'Old Course.'" Here's the last paragraph:

> St. Andrews is many things to many people: a lovely village, a university town, a proud guardian of Scottish history, but most of all the cradle of golf, which was played there in the Twelfth Century. There are endless legends of the beginnings of golf when the game was played with homemade sticks and feather (later gutta percha) balls. It is even said in St. Andrews that the word "caddy" derives from the French cadets in the court of Mary Queen of Scots, and that these little boys used feather plumes to mark the spot for a ball hit by one of the Royal Court.[7]

◆ ◆ ◆

Although gatherings at Rosemary were more formal than I'd have liked (I wanted something cozier, something like the family in "Father Knows Best"), from this distance I can see that love was there, hidden behind a handshake, a five-dollar bill, and a tale well-told.

Rosemary still stands at the end of Grand Boulevard on the Tallahatchie River. In the 1980s, while invited to be a scholar on board for a Delta bus tour, I was traveling down Grand Boulevard in Greenwood, and I remarked almost inaudibly, "That's my grandparents' house." One of the participants, a young Black student, asked me to repeat what I'd just said. Wary of what he'd think of me and my grandparents' stately home, I didn't repeat it. But he wouldn't let it go. "You have to claim it, you know," he said. So now, forty years later I guess I will. I have.

Chapter 11

Those Absent

Though the conversations at Rosemary were lively, sadness was the undercurrent though never openly acknowledged. Sadness for the three who were absent, Zilpha, Jimmy, and Bobby. Zilpha, the third child, died at age two. No one ever mentioned her in my presence. Sadly, I know no stories about her. Her marker is in the Garrard plot in Indianola, along with Grandmother's, Granddaddy's, and Grandmother's parents. So is Bobby's, the youngest son, who served in the Navy and survived the war but was killed six years later in a one-car accident. Whether it was truly an accident, posttraumatic stress, or survivor's guilt, we'll never know.

For Jimmy, the second child, the plot holds only a marker. He was lost in action while serving in the Army Air Force in World War II, and his body was never found. We have many poignant letters he wrote home. Mabelle and Mary Jayne collected them in a book they titled *Allegiance*, a choice they explain in the foreword:

> . . . all the best titles were taken: *War and Remembrance*, *Valor in Arms*, *The Unvanquished* and so on. Therefore we have given the title Allegiance to these letters, for through them comes the message of a young airman's allegiance to his family, his homeland and the free world. We think it is a story worth hearing and worth remembering.[1]

Because Jimmy was twenty-nine when he enlisted and had a wife and two small children, he was ranked a staff sergeant with no hope of promotion and assigned to be a tail gunner with the 44th Bomb Group, 8th Air Force. Despite the dangers he faced, his letters were always optimistic. They show that though he believed in and felt a deep *allegiance* to the cause for which he fought, he longed to be reunited with his family and lived for their letters and photographs. Whether written in prose, poetic form, or descriptive passages of imagined scenes at home, his sense of humor abides.

He might possibly have been the only patron at a bar ever to worry about the bartender and write a poem about him. Here are two stanzas (out of eight) from a poem called "Set'em Up, Joe":

> It matters not the aches and pains and hardships he
>   endures
> He won't tell you all his troubles though you always
>   tell him yours.
> And if the weather's hot or cold or turns from rain to
>   snow,
> It's up to you to tell him, he's not supposed to know.
>
> Should he sit down to read the news, some fool with
>   half a jag
> Pulls up a chair beside him and starts to chew the rag.
> Though Job they say had patience, a more patient
>   man by far
> Than Job could ever hope to be, is "the Man Behind
>   the Bar."

He ends the poem with these lines: "When St. Peter sees him coming, / he'll leave the gates ajar / For he knows he's had his hell on earth, / the Man Behind the Bar."[2]

At the beginning of the war, Jimmy wrote separate letters to family members, to his wife, Ethel, their two daughters, Charlotte and Mimi, his mother, father, two sisters, and two brothers. But as the war heated up, he often wrote them jointly, addressing them "Dear Folks." In the first paragraph of a letter to his daughters when stationed in England dated September 22, 1942, he writes:

> Dear Cha Cha and Mimi,
>
> How are you getting along? I can't write much about what I'm doing or where I am, because all mail is censored. I can say I am somewhere in England. We had a grand trip over, but not nearly as grand as the one home will be.

Still in England, on November 27, 1942, he writes:

> Dear Folks,
>
> I can't wait to get the pictures of Daddy and Mother. A lot of the boys Xmas packages have arrived. Mine probably will before you get this. When you don't get any from me, don't think its because I forgot any one of you. I think of you all constantly. Its just that there are so few things you can buy over here without coupons. I hope I never spend another Xmas away from home, but I guess I should be thankful I'm not spending it in a trench. This should reach you a few days before Xmas, so here's to all of you the very best, and may 1943 bring peace—a peace that's more fascinating than war. For us to have continued peace, every man on earth must be satisfied with it. One man can make war, but it takes 2 billion men, women and children to make peace.

In a letter that would be strange to the uninformed, Jimmy writes to his wife, Ethel: "The last I heard from you, you still owed the

$33 or there abouts on the new note in interest and about $20 on the old one." Ethel knew she didn't have these debts. She knew that the numbers in his highly redacted letter indicated his latitude and longitude in the Libyan desert.

In his last letter on July 1, 1943, he writes to Ethel:

> I always wanted a Mediterranean cruise but I never expected to make one in a bomber . . . Where we swim in a little rocked-in cove about 200 yards across. . . . It's 14 to 30 feet deep and so clear you can read a newspaper on the bottom. It is as gorgeous a blue as any sky you ever saw, and speaking of skies, you should see the skies out here at night. The stars seem so big you feel as though you could reach out and touch them.

Jimmy was lost in action after he volunteered for this last mission over the Libyan desert. He died in the serene blue waters he'd described.

He had already been awarded the Air Medal with three Oak Leaf clusters, a Purple Heart, and he was in line for the Distinguished Flying Cross when he died. On August 9, 1970, Garrard Hall at Keesler Air Force Base in Biloxi, Mississippi, was dedicated to him. Keesler itself was named for Second Lieutenant Samuel Reeves Keesler Jr., who was killed in France in WWI and was the brother of Jimmy's widow, Ethel.

When Jimmy's body could not be found in the Mediterranean Sea, the adjutant general sent Grandmother the telegram every mother of a serviceman or woman dreads to receive:

> I regret to inform you that the commanding general middle eastern area reports your son staff sergeant James M Garrard missing in action since two July. If further details or other

information of his status are received, you will be promptly notified.

My patriotic grandmother would have fully felt the meaning in the tradition when she traded the blue star in her window for a gold one.

Col. Leon Johnson, who was with Jimmy in the fatal crash, wrote his condolences to my grandparents and ended with: "I am terribly sorry that I can't send you better news than this. I do want to add that during the months I saw your son in action he performed his duties in a superior manner. He assisted in the safe return of our planes on numerous occasions."

To end this chapter I can do no better than the way Mary Jayne and Mabelle ended their collection—with a poem by William Alexander Percy:

> For these that come, come not forspent with years,
> Nor bent with long despair, not weak with tears.
> They mount superbly thro' the gold-flecked air.
> The light of immolation in their eyes,
> The green of youth eternal in their hair,
> And Honor's music on them like sunrise.[3]

Chapter 12

"Politest Boy in School"

As important as it is to see my father in relation to his forebears, he cannot be understood without knowing his relationship to his brother Jimmy. They were "Irish twins," eleven months apart, and inseparable. When they were two and three, Grandmother commissioned an artist, Robert Root, to paint their portrait. He portrayed them as cherubs with angel wings and posed them like Raphael's angels in the Sistine Madonna.

When guests notice the painting, now hanging in my dining room, I like to tell them that the little boys once had wings, and I point out the faint traces that are still visible. I tell them that the boys must have been particularly devilish that day to provoke Grandmother into picking up a paintbrush and painting out their wings.

That is one possibility. Maybe Grandmother wanted real boys, not cherubs. If that's true, she got what she asked for. They were always in trouble. Daddy told me that when he was only a toddler, he picked a big bouquet of flowers in a neighbor's yard. When he presented it to his mother, he was crushed when she scolded him and sent him back to the lady's house to apologize.

When they were adolescents, Granddaddy sent Daddy and Jimmy to various prep schools—Culver, Baylor, and Princeton Prep—to instill discipline. They hated being away from home and ran away every time they were sent off and hitchhiked home, only to be sent away again. In a letter to Mabelle from Princeton Prep,

Daddy describes how he and other homesick southern boys coped in their history classes way up north: "We open our books to a picture of the Confederate flag and wave at them gayly all period. It's a hot class."

Legend has it that one night Daddy and Jimmy went to a dance in nearby Rosedale (Mississippi), known for its fabled performers—W.C. Handy among them. Before they could enter the dance hall, they were lured away by a crap shoot next door—the gamblers were African American. Forgetting about the dance, Daddy and Jimmy joined in. This would have been in the 1920s, a time when "mixing the races" was strictly prohibited. The two young White boys were promptly arrested for breaking the color barrier and whisked off to jail. Without a penny in his pocket, Jimmy charmed the bailiff into releasing him to procure bail money and guaranteed his return by leaving Daddy in jail as collateral. But instead of seeking bail money, Jimmy found a tractor and chain and pulled down the wall standing between Daddy and freedom. The anecdote gives a small hint about their regard for the truth and a big one about their imaginations.

Before Jimmy enlisted, he and Daddy had a brief business partnership, Garrard Brothers, a cotton brokerage in Greenwood. If Jimmy had lived, I don't know if this enterprise would have been successful, but I do know the two brothers would have had a lot of fun.

Because Daddy was head of a cotton farming operation and because cotton was critical to the war effort, he was not drafted to serve in World War II. When Jimmy was lost in action, Daddy never got over the loss. Survivor's guilt, among other things.

Daddy was always a ready stand-in for those husbands and fathers missing or absent. When the father in the family of our neighbor across the street went overseas to serve in the Korean War, his little boy, only two at the time, called my father "Daddy," and

Daddy gladly took on the role. When Daddy's niece Charlotte, Jimmy's daughter, asked him to present her at her debut, nothing could have pleased him more.

* * *

My father looked a lot like his daddy, except that Daddy's eyes were blue, and Granddaddy's were brown. Like Granddaddy, he stood only about 5'4". They both had a full head of wavy hair, similar noses, slightly bulbous. Daddy always wore a brimmed hat when going out—never inside.

My grandfather's success as a businessman meant that Daddy had a lot to live up to—or thought he did. Being the first-born and the only surviving son and the progeny of Garrards I-IV put enormous pressure on him to succeed. He followed the plan Granddaddy had laid out for him to be a successful "planter," the term once used to describe farmers with significant land holdings. He had competent managers, a foreman who ran the gin, an accountant, and Black laborers to pick the cotton, harvest the soybeans, and tend to a small herd of cattle. He seemed to love what he did. His employees, Black and White, considered him a fair boss.

A letter from Mabelle dated April 5, 1944, sheds light on Daddy's role as eldest son:

> I'm sorry that you were out last night so I didn't get to talk to you, but I just wanted to congratulate you on your latest laurels—Chamber of Commerce & Delta Council. It seems that every time I pick up a paper these days your name is in it for one reason or another, and any day now it wouldn't be a surprise to find you marching right behind Daddy into Time magazine. You have gone further in the past five years than a lot of men go in a lifetime.

In a letter to Daddy, Mary Jayne wrote a note dated September 23, 1958, less than a month after the death of their father on August 25:

> Sitting down this morning to write notes of appreciation, it struck me the first should go to Daddy's best friend, Billy Garrard, whose loyalty and devotion to him should be an inspiration to every father and to every son.
>
> ... You, Billy, are about the last master of the Beau Geste, one of the few truly sporting people I've ever known, a man whose stature can be measured by the height of the nets. Destiny on the other side. In short, you are the answer to Mary's question "What is a gentleman?" What more could anyone want?

◆ ◆ ◆

Despite all the preparatory schools, Daddy was not a student. He attended Ole Miss for only a year yet remained one of its staunchest supporters. He was not a reader. In their courtship days while he was in New Orleans and Mother was in Pass Christian, he'd write time and again of his plans to stay home and read a book only to end up going out on the town.

Though he often left books unread, he knew how to throw out an allusion. If Mother kept him waiting, he'd stand at the door dejectedly and say, "I could've read *War and Peace* by now." He never learned a foreign language but made up a convincing phrase for goodbye. "Boulie von," he'd say when one of us was leaving, which may or may not have meant "bon voyage."

When I was little, he never gave me a spanking but corrected me sweetly by reciting:

There was a little girl
Who had a little curl
Right in the middle of her forehead.
When she was good, she was very, very good,
But when she was bad she was horrid.

Which, I've discovered, is true of most people.

In my rummaging, I found a playful telegram that suggests Daddy's appreciation for wordplay. It is from him to Mother who was visiting Ganny and Gandaddy at the Edwards Hotel and dated July 12, 1941. He says:

PRESENCE PM PENDING PISTONS PERMITTING PER YELLOW PICKUP PERHAPS=PLOVE PILLY.

He remembered lines from books and poems he might or might not have read. A favorite of his was the first line of du Maurier's *Rebecca*: "Last night I dreamt I went to Manderley again." I wish I'd asked him what it meant to him. He often quoted the famous line from Browning, "Ah but a man's reach should exceed his grasp / Or what's a heaven for?" I hope he saw it was true of him, having tried so hard to measure up to his father.

• • •

I don't know about alcoholism in my father's family. I know that Grandmother and Granddaddy were teetotalers. To abstain in the Mississippi Delta is so unusual it makes me wonder why. Was it in reaction to someone who had a problem with it, possibly Granddaddy's father, the journalist who died at thirty-one?

Apparently, the gene skipped me. I have tried sobriety, a logical outcome of my history, but it felt more a reaction than a choice.

What works for me is drinking in moderation, and I realize I am fortunate that I can do that.

I see many contributing factors to Daddy's addiction—standing in the shadow of Granddaddy's success, his exemption from war and survivor's guilt after losing both brothers to it, the hard-drinking Delta culture, and one more thing. He was head of a plantation, a system that oppressed (and still oppresses) African Americans. Whether his drinking increased his blindness or his blindness increased his drinking, I don't know.

• • •

The trouble with a blind spot is you can't see it. Most of the White people in that time and place wore such blinders, me included. We thought we'd done pretty well to transition from slavery to sharecropping and then paying wages, paltry though they were. The rationalizations warped us.

Here's an image that broke my heart years ago and still does. It's a quilt stitched by an African American woman artist, Gwen Magee. The scene is a cotton field on a sunny day. In the bottom right corner, the backs of Black laborers bend unnaturally as they pull cotton from prickly bolls and drag heavy sacks behind them. In the top left corner, a couple pass by in an open car. The passenger holds a pink umbrella, completely obscuring the field of laborers. The open car suggests the couple's desire to see the countryside while the pink umbrella obstructs the view they don't want to see.

When Daddy was going around town, checking on things at the Compress, going by the bank to charm the tellers, or telling stories to his buddies at Weber's Truck Stop, he was Charming Billy. But from time to time, out of the blue, he'd get choked up over something. He'd cover it up with a laugh even as tears filled his eyes. Something within him knew that things weren't right, but he didn't try or wasn't equipped to explore why.

He was kind to me, gentle. Whenever I was leaving, he'd escort me to the car. Even when he was aging, he would insist on carrying my luggage. When I thanked him, his eyes twinkled as he murmured "politest boy in school," the designation given him in his high school yearbook. Because of his gentleness, I found it difficult to hold him responsible for my unhappiness. Like many other sons and daughters, I found it easier to blame Mother.

He served on several local boards, the local bank, an animal rescue operation, the Girl Scouts and was president of the Rotary Club, the country club, the Sunflower Compress, and Delta Council, a prestigious organization then and now. (William Faulkner was the speaker at the Delta Council meeting in the spring of 1952.) But by the time I came along, Daddy's drinking was already taking its toll, his activities had slowed down, and he'd begun his decline.

But affection never did, his for others, ours for him. Here's an unsigned poem that could have been written by Mabelle or Mary Jayne:

Of Brothers

You can have the Karamazovs
And the coughless brothers Smith;
As for me, I'll opt for Billy
As the brother to be with.

Adele Astair had Freddy,
Each cadet a Brother Rat;
But they were missing something,
For Billy's where-it's-at.

Oh, Orville's bag was Wilbur;
And in the hood of brothers
Sing the praises, if you like,
Of Kennedys or Smothers.

But when the shouting's finished
For these and all the rest,
I'll still be making book on
Our Billy for the best.

Reading Daddy's love letters to Mother, his letters to family members, and others' recollections of him has given me a fuller sense of what a loved and loving man he was. He was the one who invited Ganny to live with us. Letters from Granddaddy—to whom Daddy never felt equal—never express in words his deep love for his son and respect for the work he did. But Granddaddy couldn't say it, and Daddy couldn't see it. In the letter already quoted from Mabelle to Daddy dated April 5, 1944, she says:

> Of all the compliments I could pay you, though, I'm sure the one you'd prefer is that you're a real chip off the old block.
>
> Anything I could say to you would be what Jimmy and Mary Jayne and Bobby would say if they were here, so I'll just say that having Daddy for our father and you for our brother, we were dealt aces back to back.

Chapter 13

"Flapper, Yes, She's One of Those"

For most of my life I have tried to find the key to Mother's personality. From what I know, she had an ideal childhood with stable, economically secure parents, industrious, middle class, and down to earth. She had many friends and belonged to a close-knit community.

Born in 1910, Mary Lucile Clark was the only girl in a family of five children. She was nicknamed "Teeny," a diminutive that she seemed to like. Her brothers adored her and always included her in their activities. They all liked playing the ukulele and accompanying each other to popular songs of the day, "Yes, Sir, That's My Baby," "Harvest Moon," "Don't Bring Lulu," and "For Me and My Gal."

She was "five foot two," as another popular song goes from that era. [See Addendum C.] The song describes her not only physically but also the carefree attitude (or the façade of a carefree attitude) of the times.

Mother grew up in Tupelo. Although only 150 miles apart, the hill town of Tupelo was extremely different from the Delta town of Indianola. Incorporated in 1870, Tupelo was built *after* the Civil War, significant because it meant that the Whites living there escaped the guilt, shame, and resentment that Whites in towns like Indianola carried, whether they knew it or not. By then the removal of the Chickasaw tribe had become a faint memory to the White inhabitants of Tupelo. (Most of the Chickasaw tribe had been removed to Indian Territory by 1851.) In many ways, Tupelo was less traumatized and I want to say more wholesome than Indianola and other towns in the Delta. And yet Delta people felt superior to "hill people," a contradiction that Freud or Jung might understand.

In the archive of my secretary, I found three letters to Ganny from Mother at fifteen. In a photograph of her at about this time, she has light brown, wavy hair, and an open look. Her eyes are bright, and her smile is easy.

The letters were written to Ganny in New York in 1925. Mother's letters are filled with references to her best friend, Frances Elkin, their close friendship made closer because their mothers were also best friends, and Frances's father, Dr. Elkin, was the family doctor.

In the first letter, postmarked from Tupelo on January 25, 1925, she and Frances both write and sign the letter. The letter is addressed to:

Mrs. R.B. Clark
The Astor Hotel
New York, NY

Sunday afternoon, 5:30 O'clock

Dear Muddy and Cousin May,

I hope you get there allright or rather will <u>get</u> there allright. I will write you a long letter tomorrow but Frances and myself wanted an excuse to go to the Post office (we had a hard time finding the stamp, too.) We sure do miss you.

Love,
Teeny and Frances

The second one was postmarked from Tupelo the next day, January 26, 7 p.m., 1925. It was addressed to Ganny (Muddy) at the Astor Hotel:

Monday aft.

Dear Muddy,

Here is what happened after you left us Saturday night.

Daddy brought us home but he had to go back to the bank. We started cracking hickory nuts and Cousin Grace told us a continued story she had been reading and I got so interested in it I started it and she read the last number. Poor Johnnie didn't have anything to do but to go to bed. The name of it is "Bobbed Hair." Have you read any of it?

Sunday

I got up right early because I had a new dress to put on. Everybody thought it was pretty and Daddy thought it was the prettiest one I had! I sure did have one big surprise. Daddy said, "I think your legs look pretty in those stockings." I was kinder surprised but I said, "Do you?" He said, "You know, if I were you, I would put on stockings all the time. I don't think you are too big to wear socks if you want to but I think you are big enough to wear stockings." It nearly took my breath away.

Sunday afternoon I went around to Frances'ses. We were just getting ready to walk around and act silly when Tot came in. We were so mad. Then after a while Ruth and Grace R. came in and we played Miss Irene Blair and all the others. Then we went out doors and played throwing the statue and blind mans bluff. After the others had gone home Frances and myself walked around and mailed the note to you. We call ourselves the "Sunday gad-abouts." I went to the League that night and then we went to church. (Rebecca went to sleep in church.)

Monday

I sure did hate to get up this morning. Daddy took us to school in the car. I took a music lesson the second period and when I got through I told Miss Weaver I might have to stop when we moved out in the country. She like to had a fit. She said it wouldn't hurt so much for anybody who wasn't talented but she said it would be a shame for me to stop! I was thrilled pink and when I told Frances she was jealous green. I had another funny thing to happen to me today. Miss Davis never does brag on anybody. But today Frances and myself had just made Cream of Tomato Soup. When she tasted it we just expected her to say "It's alright," like she always does but she said "Its good, its real good!" I wish I had liked it so I could have gotten the benefit of it.

This afternoon Frances made me walk to T.K.E. twice, Bunche's, Weatherall's, Davis'es, Broken Doller Store, St. Clair, Mississippi Store, The Bank, and even to a place where they sold horse stuff, hunting for a certain kind of notebook she wanted!

And now I am at home writing this letter.

Daddy is going to take Cousin Grace and me to the show tomorrow night.

If you get time please get me a piece of music called "The grass is always greener" (In the other fellow's yard) That's the way it looks. Miss Weaver taught it to us and it sure is cute.

Don't any of us know what to do without you so please hurry home fast Muddy.

Lots and lots of Love, Teeny

P.S. I made 75 on my exam, Grace made 83 & Ruth made 63.

The third letter is postmarked Tupelo, June 15, 1925, and is addressed to Ganny at Pennsylvania Hotel in New York. The reference to "Obbie's girl" indicates that Ganny has gone to New York to see her oldest son and meet his girlfriend.

> Dear Muddy,
>
> I expect this letter will be there when you get there but I want you to be sure and get it. After we left you last nite we rode out on the west concrete roads and then circled on around by the old Calhoun place. When we got up there about at the Dairy Cousin Grace noticed that it looked like there was a fire in town. So we began guessing where it was. Cousin Grace guessed it was Turner's planing saw-mill, Daddy guessed it was Mr. Sim Hind's, I guessed it was near Aunt Dells and John guessed all over town. After we got closer Daddy decided positively that it was Turner's Mill. I think he even said he could see the lumber burning. It turned out to be the Hollaway's house. You know they had just moved to Memphis. But when Daddy discovered it he said, "it's just exactly where I thought it was, right at Mr. Sim Hinds!" It was a pretty bad fire but I don't know whether it burnt to the ground or not.
>
> I hope you saw Obbie's girl but please hurry home.
>
> Lots and lots of love, Teeny.
>
> P.S. You will have a check at Weatheralls waiting for you for a box of stationary and a bottle of ink when you come back. Hope you don't mind very much. Teeny

I love these letters. I love her in this phase of her life, so excited and full of life, and how I wish it had continued.

My mother, Mary Lucile Clark, at age fifteen

In another photograph of Mother, this time as a young adult, her looks have changed. No longer is she the wholesome-looking fifteen-year-old. Now her eyebrows are arched and plucked severely, her lipstick is dark and painted in a bow, her hair is bobbed in the crimped waves of Greta Garbo or Clara Bow.

Mother came of age at the end of the Roarin' Twenties, the flapper era, and in many ways, she never left it. Like other women of her era, she rebelled against the restrictions of the previous Victorian era (and who wouldn't?). She wanted freedom to drink if she wanted to, smoke if she wanted to, dance if she wanted to, and go where she wanted to without a chaperone. And why shouldn't she? The pendulum had swung. I wonder if Ganny, who'd had to repress so much, was secretly proud of her. But sooner or later, we grow up and assume responsibilities. Mother never fully assumed hers.

After Mother died, her friend Frances Elkin Joiner brought me a stack of letters Mother wrote her. In a handwritten note enclosed with the letters, Frances says, "We were always 'in love' with some boy, and her letters are full of some special one at the moment! Some are more than she might want me to pass on—cute as can be, but just raving—as I'm sure mine to her were." *Raving*. Boy crazy. In short, a flapper.

The letters between Frances and Mother began in their college years when Frances was at National Park Seminary in Forest Glen, Maryland, and Mother was a seventeen-year-old at Ole Miss. They continue after Mother transferred to Mississippi State College for Women (MSCW—now MUW) and Newcomb College in New Orleans. After Frances leaves for college, Mother writes about the pain of being separated from her, how sad it was to pass by Frances's house without Frances in it, and concludes, "I just have to tell you now, that I love you better than any girl in the whole world and always will."

In her letters to Frances after arriving at MSCW, Mother does seem "raving" in writing about her crush on a young man named Connie and soon after about another one named Gene:

> Connie!! Oh I just can't even think about him. He was so sweet last nite—was it last nite? Seems ages ago. But I still am not sure that he cares anything about me—and I worship him.

When she forgets about these beaus, she laughs at herself in an endearing way. From MSCW, she reports to Frances that immediately after being chosen "Most Graceful," she stumbled *ungracefully* when a fellow student congratulated her.

After Mother received a degree from Newcomb College, she writes Frances that she's met a man different from the rest:

> I haven't been doing anything much, except I had the best time I ever had in my life when I went to Greenwood with Billy Labor Day week-end. He has the cutest family I ever saw in my life, two sisters, 21 & 19 yrs. old, and two brothers, 23 & 13, and they are every one just as crazy as Billy is. Mr. & Mrs. Garrard are just adorable. I never have fallen so completely in love with a family. And they live in a perfectly enormous house & it's full of servants.

In her last letter to Frances, written on April 10, 1934, Mother tells Frances that she and Billy are going to marry and that she has broken it off with her old beau Gene Thompson, who had also proposed.

Then she delivers a blow. She says the wedding will have to be only the immediate family. She says she has begged her parents to let her include Frances, but they persuaded her otherwise, reasoning that excluded relatives would be hurt.

The decision caused a rift between Mother and her best friend. When Frances brought me Mother's letters, she assured me there were no hard feelings on her end. For that I was grateful. But I knew that Mother had caused it because I'd seen many times how she put Daddy's relatives before her own and her new Delta friends before the old ones in Tupelo. To her detriment and to mine. I barely knew my Tupelo kin or Mother's old friends.

• • •

In 1985, when Frances learned of my friendship with my colleague, Dorothy Shawhan, a native of Verona who grew up in Tupelo, she invited us to come for a weekend at her home in Tupelo. With no reference to their rift, she told me only good stories about Mother. She drove us around and showed us all the old haunts Mother

My father, William Montjoy Garrard V, at age twenty-one

mentions in her letters, T.K.E., Bunches, and Weatheralls, or rather where they once were. Most of these places had been swept away by the deadly tornado that hit Tupelo in 1936.

It was a bittersweet tour but a delightful weekend. Frances's daughter, also named Frances, was soon to be married, and that first night we all sat around the dining room table tying rice into bundles with blue ribbon for the wedding. I came away with my hunch reinforced that Tupelo was and is a wholesome town and that the Delta had not been good for Mother. I also mourned, on Mother's behalf, the loss of her friendship with a dear and remarkable woman.

Chapter 14

Love Letters

Reading letters back-to-back from Daddy to his sister Mabelle when he was at Ole Miss and the ones from Mother to Frances, I was struck by how much alike they sounded, both full of life, gossip, and romantic ideas. Daddy gave Mabelle advice about playing it cool with boys and told her not to write a beau too often, while Mother complained to Frances about a boy who wrote only once a week.

When they met, Daddy was living in New Orleans and working for the Federal Compress. After he took the job, he planned on spending his first night with Aunt Marion (Grandmother's sister) and her husband, Dr. Jimmy Rives, before finding an apartment, but he ended up staying with them for a year, an arrangement that apparently suited all of them. Because of the closeness that developed between them, Aunt Marion and Uncle Jimmy would play a big part in all our lives. For all our medical questions, we called Uncle Jimmy, a surgeon at Touro Infirmary, or Aunt Marion, a nurse before they married. Aunt Marion is, in fact, the reason I'm here. When Mother had difficulty conceiving me, she asked Aunt Marion for advice, and whatever it was worked. My grateful mother then named me for her.

In the early 1930s, shortly after Mother finished her degree at Newcomb, Mother, Ganny, and Gandaddy lived for a time in Pass Christian, Mississippi. I can imagine they were cautiously keeping

Mother and Daddy apart until they married. And from the many letters they wrote to each other during that time of gas shortages and lack of cash, sixty miles were more than enough to keep them apart.

The letters between them were passionate. At times Daddy's to her were desperately romantic while Mother's were more restrained. In almost every letter, Daddy says, "I cannot stand to be without you another minute" and "I can't get you out of my mind." He says the words "I love you" first, and, maybe to play it cool or keep the upper hand, Mother won't say them, even when Daddy asks her to. But in her own time, she does so and agrees to marry him.

When Daddy tells his boss at Federal Compress that he is getting married, he gives Daddy a raise and relocates him to the Federal Compress in Shaw, Mississippi, a booming business at the time. Mother and Daddy begin making wedding plans, and Daddy looks for a place for them to live. He tells her to tell her mother not to worry, that she'll be safe in Shaw and that it has a movie theatre and a bank. For a moviegoer who also didn't mind spending money, what more could she ask for?

Daddy finds a contractor who agrees to build a house to their specifications and then rent it to them, a sweet deal. And that's when trouble begins. Daddy tells Mother he's picked out which of the two bedrooms will be theirs. Mother is furious and lets him have it. She tells him if he's going to be so bossy, maybe she'll sleep in her own room or not marry him at all!

He writes back immediately, contrite and full of apologies. He sends her the house plans and asks for her ideas. Later she apologizes for the "mean" letter she wrote earlier but continues to keep the upper hand.

Reminiscent of the lovers in O'Henry's "Gift of the Magi," she urges him to take up reading, hoping he will share her passion, and he sends her a tennis racket, encouraging her to take up his. (He never became an avid reader, and she never took up tennis.)

I was entranced with the letters when I first found them, and then I began to see the fault lines. In nearly every letter, Daddy alternates between describing his drinking escapades and his intentions to be more moderate, to drink beer instead of whiskey, or as she frequently suggests, to stay home and read a book. Mother tells him about getting "tight" in the middle of the day but reports that it had worn off by evening, meaning that Ganny was none the wiser. Both seem ambivalent about their drinking, a little ashamed, a little pleased.

They married on June 18, 1934, at Middlegate, a locally famous Japanese garden in Pass Christian, Mississippi, no longer there. A writer for the *Birmingham News*, wrote:

> Down a bamboo bordered path, the lovely bride, gowned in white lace with a short wedding veil, walked, escorted by her father. The groom with his best man, his brother, came along another walk, bordered with blooming shrubs, to meet his bride. Other attendants were Misses Mabelle and MaryJane Garrard, sisters of the groom, and John and Cannon Clark, brothers of the bride. . . . Mrs. Garrard is a former Tupelo girl, one of the loveliest and most popular of this city.[1]

It grieves me that no photographs were taken of the wedding. I can only guess that, in the middle of the Depression, they were too expensive.

Recently I discovered a book about the gardens called *Middlegate*, published in 2011 and written by Lynne White, a granddaughter of the original owners.[2] I was debating whether to buy this rare and expensive book when the owner of Pass Books told me he'd just bought a copy at an auction. Unable to decide if he wanted to part with it and sell it to me, he told me what he'd paid for it. "That's okay," I said. Then he made an offer I liked better—to come to his bookstore and read the book to my heart's content. It would be the next best thing to seeing photographs of the wedding.

On a day in June of 2022, close to the date of Mother and Daddy's anniversary, I went to the coast and spent the night at my sister-in-law's house in Ocean Springs before going to Pass Christian the next day. On my way to Pass Books, I was driving along the busy beach highway when I glimpsed the Gulf waters on my left. The slant of the midmorning sun made the water and sky look like a seamless whole. Without a horizon, I felt momentarily disoriented, and then I felt as if I was traveling back in time. The drive was magical and heartbreaking. It made me long for my young father and my young mother on their wedding day, as wonderfully perfect on that day as they were meant to be.

When I reached the bookstore and scanned the books on the "hold" shelf, one of the clerks looked up, and before I could say a word, she said, "I bet I know what you're looking for." She handed me the book, offered me a cup of coffee, and showed me up a spiral staircase to the quiet second story where I could read undisturbed. I opened the book. Time disappeared again as I turned the pages.

In the preface, Lynne White says that her grandfather Rudolph S. Hecht came to America from Ansbach, Germany, to find work and eventually became a banker in New Orleans. He came to Pass Christian to stay at a resort called Lynne Castle, owned by Lin and Estella Watkins and considered one of the most aristocratic hotels on the coast. There he met the Watkins's daughter, Lynne, and was so smitten by her that he left behind an important document so that he'd have an excuse to see her again. They married in 1911. After Lynne Castle burned in 1915, Estella Watkins built another resort and divided it into three parts, "Westgate," "Middlegate," and "Eastgate." They rented out rooms at Westgate and Eastgate. Middlegate was transformed into gardens inspired by those Estella had seen on a trip to Japan. Lynne Watkins Hecht, who'd studied pottery at Newcomb College under the eminent professor William Woodward, helped her mother design them. Construction began in the 1920s.

The photographs of Middlegate gardens are in themselves works of art. They are arranged in the order they'd have been seen on entering the garden. At the entry is a bright red lacquered torii gate flanked by a pair of protective porcelain Fu dogs. Ceramic egrets dot the landscape. Inside, a fountain shimmers above a wide pond, a wishing well sits atop a bridge, and a Tea House with a blue tiled roof stands above a waterfall. A Wishing Bridge on a pond makes a half-circle that is completed by its reflection in the water. Overlooking the grounds and dominating the landscape stands a bronze Buddha statue. Made in 1735 A.D., it was an astounding twelve feet high and weighed 5,750 pounds.

In 1926 one of the first known gatherings at Middlegate took place. The occasion was to honor a prominent couple, Mr. and Mrs. Henry Luce. He was the founder of both *Time* and *Life*. She was a well-known U.S. ambassador, politician, and writer. Many parties and weddings followed.

Mother and her parents rented an apartment at Eastgate while in Pass Christian. I know this because the addresses on Daddy's letters to Mother in the spring of 1934 are all addressed to her at 514 West Beach Boulevard, which was Eastgate.

As President of the Federal Land Bank in New Orleans, my grandfather Clark would have been acquainted with Lynn Watkins Hecht's husband, who was president of the New Orleans branch of Hibernia Bank. But the Clarks must have been surprised when, on hearing their plans for a wedding, Mr. Hecht offered them Middlegate, free of charge. Mother writes to Daddy:

> But this is the grand part—He just insisted to Daddy and me, too, that I must have the ceremony in the Japanese garden,

> and said just plan to have it anyway that I wanted to! I'm so excited over that and I think he's the sweetest, most thoughtful man I've ever seen. Muddy and I thought that since it's to be in the Garden the best time to have it would be late in the afternoon, or even maybe at night with lights strung around.

The gardens were severely damaged by Hurricane Camille in 1969 and destroyed by Hurricane Katrina in 2005.

◆ ◆ ◆

In many ways, Mother and Daddy were a good match. In a letter Mary Jayne said they were "her ideal couple." Mother adored Daddy's family, he adored hers, and all the siblings liked each other as well. But the romantic wedding at Middlegate may have increased their already high expectations and illusions about marriage. From what I observed, their marriage never evolved from the romantic stage to a more mature, mutually satisfying partnership.

The flapper in Mother said she could have it all, but the culture said no. The contradiction shows up in a photo taken of Mother after she married. She looks matronly. Her cheeks are rouged. Her lips are a dark red but undefined. Her slight smile looks forced. Her eyes are unfocussed. She wears a plain white blouse with a pale blue ribbon trailing from the collar.

Mother seemed to expect Daddy to fulfill her every need. She was furious if he stayed on the golf course longer than she preferred. Even though she was financially dependent on him, she expected a full partnership. Yet they were partners in only one activity, their drinking. They were social drinkers at first with a wide circle of friends to party with, but as their drinking progressed, their friends became less necessary, and after a while they were a party of two.

Chapter 15

The Delta, Part One

Mother was swept away not only by Daddy, his family, and the house full of servants at Rosemary but by the Delta itself. It is a land so flat that you can see all the way to the horizon. You look up and see a great big blue bowl of sky or stars so close that you forget all worldly concerns. Crops grow magically in the lush, fertile soil. With Nature so near, you feel and resonate with her slow rhythm. Scores of writers have been smitten by this mysterious place called the Delta.

On a long, hot summer afternoon when I was fourteen or fifteen, I was bored. Nothing to do. No school, no friends at home, nothing. Finding Mother in the library, I sat on the ottoman, elbows on knees, chin cupped in hand, and complained about the boring weather, the boring town, the boring people. "I'm bored to tears," I muttered. She got up, went over to the bookshelves, took down Eudora Welty's *Delta Wedding*, and handed it to me. "Try this," she said. "It's about the Delta."

"Our Delta?" I said casually, pretending disinterest. Within minutes, I was captivated because the title promised to be not only about the Delta but a wedding! Thanks to my mother's astuteness and Miss Welty's imagination, my people, my town, my Delta would never again be boring to me.

And then there's William Alexander Percy. Few writers have captured as eloquently a sense of his time and place than this poet and memoirist. The first chapter of his memoir, *Lanterns on the Levee* (1941), is called "The Delta." He says: "My country is the Mississippi Delta, the river country. It lies flat, like a badly drawn half oval, with Memphis at its northern and Vicksburg at its southern tip."[1] He gives a vivid if rosy picture of the culture he knew. Through his eyes even the crude dance floor at the Greenville Elysian Club became . . .

> thoroughly entrancing when Handy appeared and the dancing started. Delta girls are born dancing and never stop, which is as it should be, for surely it is the finest form of human amusement except tennis and talking. The club's dances were famous from Hushpuckna to Yazoo City, and they were the right sort of affairs, with rows of broad-bosomed lares and penates against the wall and so many good-looking animated girls drawling darkest Southernese and doing intricate steps by instinct or inspiration that no one could think of going home before daylight.[2]

Though nonfiction, the book reads like poetry. The last sentence is one of my favorites: "The sound of the river-boats hangs inside your heart like a star."[3]

W.A. Percy's second cousin, adopted son, and protégé, Walker Percy, has another, quite different, description of the Delta. In his novel, *The Last Gentleman*, when protagonist Will Barrett finally arrives in a thinly disguised Delta town of Greenville (Mississippi) after a long pilgrimage from New York, the narration begins:

> Down flew the Trave-L-Aire into the setting sun, down and out of the last of the ancient and impoverished South of red hills and Cardui signs and God-is-Love crosses. Down through humpy sugarloaves and loess cliffs sliced through like

> poundcake. Dead trees shrouded in kudzu vines reared up like old women. Down and out at last and onto the vast prodigal plain of the Delta, stretching away misty and fecund into the October haze. The land hummed and simmered in its own richness. Picking was still going on, great $25,000 McCormicks and Farmalls browsing up and down the cotton rows. Bugs zoomed and splashed amber against the windshield; the Trav-L-Aire pushed like a boat through the heavy air and the rich protein smells, now the sweet ferment of alfalfa, and the smell of cottonseed meal rich as ham in the kitchen.[4]

David Cohn, another protégé of W.A. Percy, with an eloquence that rivaled his mentor's, is famous for the first line of his memoir, *Where I was Born and Raised*: "The Delta begins in the lobby of the Peabody Hotel and ends at Catfish Row in Vicksburg."[5] In one line, he gives the reader not only a playful geographical map but also suggests a state of mind.

In Tennessee Williams's plays, the Delta is sometimes portrayed as if it is another character, fertile, sexual, and hypnotic. As reckless, sensuous Carol Cutrere describes in *Orpheus Descending*, "there's something wild" about it.

Born and raised in Yazoo City, a town with one foot in the hills and one in the Delta, Willie Morris exuberantly describes the Delta this way in his memoir *North Toward Home*:

> Beyond these hills, if you follow the highway as it forks north and slightly west, the hills suddenly come to an end and there is one long, final descent. Out in the distance, as far as the eye can see, the land is flat, dark, and unbroken, sweeping away in a faint misty haze to the limits of the horizon. This is the great delta. Once it was the very floor under the sea; later knee-deep in waters and covered with primordial forests—a

> dank shadowy swampland, fetid and rich. There will not be a hill or a rise now until just below Memphis, 180 miles away. In a fast car a man can almost make it to Tennessee on automatic pilot, driving the straight, level road in a kind of euphoria, past the cotton fields and the tenant shacks, the big plantation houses and the primitive little Negro churches, over the muddy creeks and rivers through the counties with the forgotten Indian names—Leflore, Coahoma, Tallahatchie, Tunica.[6]

In her library, my mother had books by these writers and more. Anybody who reads their descriptions of the Delta could fall for its glamour. I know I did.

Chapter 16

The Delta, Part Two

The Delta is not what it seems. The designation itself is erroneous, a misnomer. A delta is formed at a river's mouth. Ours is a floodplain created from the river's overflow.

Those who see the Delta as a place of wealth and glamour can do so only by disregarding a large portion of the population. In those days when we called King Cotton "white gold," we didn't notice the silence of the laborers who picked and hauled it. Breaking the silence would have been dangerous, so they kept quiet about their hardships and continued picking cotton "from can to caint," like their enslaved forebears.

In the 1930s two prominent scholars came to Indianola at different times and investigated these silences and wrote courageously about what they found. These two were scholars John Dollard, a sociologist and author of *Caste and Class in a Southern Town* (1937),[1] and Hortense Powdermaker, an anthropologist and author of *After Freedom* (1939).[2] Though Dollard called it "Southerntown" and Powdermaker called it "Cottonville," both were writing about a thinly disguised Indianola.

Each had chosen our town because it was small and well defined. At the time, it had fewer than 5,000 inhabitants, a manageable size for collecting data. The class system was delineated geographically by the railroad—African Americans lived to the south; Whites to the north.

Reading these books was an eye-opener for me. For the first time I understood several layers of meanings for what Eudora Welty has called "sense of place." It can mean everyone knows their place, sometimes a comfort, sometimes unfair when someone else assigns it. But if one is under threat to "stay in his place," it can be stifling or a nightmare. In the Delta, if a prominent (wealthy) planter gets drunk at the country club, he knows he won't lose his "place," that is, his status in the culture. But if a poor man (or woman) breaks the social norms, he will be punished.

Though at different times, Dollard and Powdermaker stayed in Indianola for an extended period and collected first-hand accounts from both races, Black and White, that revealed stark differences of attitude, lifestyle, and behavior some seventy years after the Civil War. Dollard lived in a White boarding house (run, coincidentally, by my husband's grandmother Kathleen Claiborne). I prefer Powdermaker's book because it is deeper and more reliable because she chose to live south of the railroad, the Black section town, and in so doing, she built trust between herself and the people she interviewed, a trust that yielded candid truths. After hundreds of interviews, Powdermaker concludes, "The average [W]hite person in this community seldom realizes the extent to which this [Black] group questions his [White] superiority."[3]

A woman Powdermaker interviewed said, "Didn't the Lord makes us all? The Whites have the power and all the advantage now, but they ain't no different from the colored folks."[4] A Black man she interviewed stated, "The Negroes always have the laugh on the Whites because the Whites are always being deceived by them, and never know it."[5]

Once Powdermaker was passing the time rocking on a porch with an elderly Black woman she designates as "Mother B." The elderly woman was cautious in her talk at first and spouted the usual patter about the good old days. But when Powdermaker unhurriedly kept rocking, another picture emerged. Mother B told Powdermaker that her father had been sold away before she was old enough to remember him and confided: "In those days people were sold like oxen and horses." No longer able to suppress her bitterness, she recalled the day of her mother's funeral when she was only a child. She couldn't understand why her brothers and sisters were allowed to go to the funeral while her mistress made her keep working.

Here's another of Powdermaker's observations:

> One woman, when asked about a recent lynching in a neighboring town, looks surprised and says she has heard nothing about it. Later she thinks perhaps she has heard something after all, but it "didn't sink in" and so she forgot it. She explains that she doesn't let herself think about lynchings any more than she can help because if she did think about them she would become bitter, and she does not want to become bitter.[6]

• • •

White attitudes about Black inferiority continued into the forties, fifties, and beyond. I remember a time in the fifties witnessing a Black woman being scolded by a White receptionist in at the optometrist's office for trying to come in the front door. I remember being in the town library when, upon seeing a Black patron reading a book, a White woman whispered to me, "I didn't know they were letting *them* in."

Indianola was the site of the first White Citizen's Council meeting in 1954. My father didn't join, thank God, because, being self-employed, he didn't have to; he was not financially dependent on the business community. A person who was dependent might lose his job, or business, or get kicked out of town if he didn't join.

Except perhaps in a few history classes, Powdermaker's and Dollard's books are not well known. Even less well known is the fact that the interviews in "Cottonville" and "Southerntown" took place in Indianola. Learning about these books and their subject left me more enlightened and more distraught.

Chapter 17

"Nothing Gold Can Stay"

Nature's first green is gold.
Her hardest hue to hold.
Her early leaf's a flower;
But only so an hour.
Then leaf subsides to leaf.
So Eden sank to grief,
So dawn goes down to day,
Nothing gold can stay.

—ROBERT FROST[1]

In a letter Mother wrote to Cannon in San Francisco on May 18, 1950, she paints a rosy picture of our family life.

Dear Cannon,

The lamb is shorn and enclosed is the evidence. [She enclosed a lock of my hair tied with a pink ribbon.] Marion is so proud of her new hair-do and really does look adorable although much older (ancient). I'm going to have some pictures made soon and will send you one.

Mary is in the throes of Junior Hi graduation and is Salutatorian, having been nosed out of Valedictorian by one point and a half. Ann [Saville's daughter] is coming for a visit the middle of June—her school isn't out til then—and then Mary is going to Camp Kittiwake at Pass Christian the first of July. We have really spent a busy spring, with Delta Council, Spelling Bees, etc. going on and I'll be glad to settle down to the dullness of summer with nothing to do but take Marion swimming every afternoon.

Billy and I wished for you in New York and reminisced about when we were there together. We saw "Gentlemen Prefer Blondes," "Detective Story," "Mr. Roberts," "I Know My Love," and "Clutterbut." With much love, Teeny

• • •

When I was about four, for reasons I don't understand, Mother and Daddy took me with them to a party at the house of the "Wilsons" down the street rather than leave me at home with Ganny. I could smell what they were drinking in the crowded kitchen where the grownups were gathered; it was the same sharp smell I hated in the doctor's office. Soon they were spilling their drinks, talking too loudly, and laughing too long. When they started acting silly, I got scared.

When "Denny" started singing, "My Bonnie Lies over the Ocean," "Herman" joined in and then whisked me up and tossed me to "Jack." The rest of the group joined in, made a circle, and tossed me from one person to the next at the end of every line of the song. "My Bonnie lies over the ocean." *Toss.* "My Bonnie lies over the sea." *Toss.* On the chorus, "Bring back, bring back, oh, bring back my Bonnie to me, to me," "Sylvie" grabbed my hands and "Denny" grabbed my feet, and they swung me wildly from side to side.

I went home with an intense mixture of feelings. I liked the attention but hated seeing Mother, Daddy, and the other adults acting so stupid. I still remember being terrified they'd drop me when they tossed me around.

Shortly after Mother painted the rosy picture of our family in her letter to Cannon, things changed. The pleasure Mother once took in watching her girls grow up evaporated. Once she lost interest in us, she didn't know what to do with herself. As the wife of a prominent planter, she had a privileged status, though nobody knew exactly what the role meant or what she was supposed to do. To her it meant she didn't need to work outside the home or *in* it. But then she could only play so much bridge, lick so many Green Stamps, embroider so many pillowcases. What *was* she supposed to do?

She began making plans for building a dream home (though she wouldn't have called it that—too kitschy). It would fill whatever was missing in her life. She hired a noted architect from Memphis to design it.

• • •

I turned my affections to Daddy. I'd ride "the place" with him most mornings before starting school. We called it that because, unenlightened though we were, we couldn't quite call it a plantation, but farm wasn't right either with its connotations of a rustic place with pigs and chickens. If "the place" was a vague term, so be it.

In my earliest memories, I am standing next to Daddy in his truck as he drives. I have one hand on his shoulder and grip a bottle of Coke in the other. Now and then we stop, get out to examine the cotton, and then meet up with his manager, Mr. Clanton, to discuss the day's business. After that, Daddy takes me with him to Weber's Truck Stop, where he orders coffee for himself, another Coke for me, and meets up with his buddies, who tease me in a friendly way. Once we're home, Daddy lets me out. He holds up his first two fingers close together and says, "Partner, we're just like that."

Me on a ride with Daddy to our lake in the pasture

Daddy loved raising cotton. He knew every step of the process from seed to market and would explain it to anybody who'd listen. In a bread-and-butter letter, Nonie, my roommate from Cathedral, mentions Daddy's patience in teaching her about cotton production from seed to square to bloom and from gin to compress to market.

In a letter Ganny wrote to Cannon in 1956, she describes going with Daddy to see the new artesian well: "It pumps 1800 gals. per minute—making a regular canal on the place. So far this is the best crop he's ever made. You'll see some of the gathering in Oct—I hope." After Cannon's visit, he writes to Mother and speaks knowledgeably about the farming operation, having also been taught by the expert, Daddy.

• • •

I had my own interest in watching the cotton grow because I hoped to win a contest held by the local newspaper every spring and summer. Whoever brought in the first square or bloom got her (or his) name in the paper. In those seasons, I'd tell Daddy to wake me up extra early. Because Daddy was as eager as I was, I think I won more than anybody.

Tromping trailers was even more fun. After the laborers had handpicked the cotton or later driven mechanical pickers, they dumped it in a long trailer and hauled it to the gin where the seed was separated from the fiber. After a go-ahead from Daddy, my friends and I would climb up the trailer's high sides, scramble over, and throw ourselves into the downy cotton. We'd squeal, get up, leap, and fall into the cushy piles of fluff and then do it all over again. If we'd known we were helping pack the cotton, we'd have asked to be paid.

• • •

There were also other pleasures. I almost went to a river baptism once. John said he'd take me, He was one of the tractor drivers, a burly, good-hearted, middle-aged Black man who drove a Jeep that he'd let me ride in from time to time. He told me that in his church, they baptized their people at sunrise in the Sunflower River. I'd recently been baptized at the White Baptist Church and hadn't liked it at all. The water was murky and smelled like chlorine. The baptismal font was enclosed by a glass side facing the congregation so all could see us getting dunked. To this day, I regret that I didn't get up in time to see a sunrise baptism.

Chapter 18

On Barberry Lane

When the new house was nearly ready, Mother and Daddy took me over to see it. They waited for my response, probably expecting squeals of excitement. "It looks cruel," I blurted. Mother assured me that it would look better after they planted shrubs and flowers. But my remark was prescient. In 1951, when we left our old house and moved into the new one, it was a cruel transition.

I'd lost the coziness of the old house, missed the room I shared with Mary that was adjacent to Ganny's. Missed the floor furnaces that warmed my legs. I'd lost my playhouse in the backyard. I'd lost my neighborhood playmates, Barbara, Henry, and the Hartness girls. The new neighborhood had no girls at all, only boys, and though I'd soon become friends with George, Jack, Joe, and Spencer, they didn't take the place of my former buddies.

After we moved into the new house, Mother fell into a deep and sudden depression. When I'd walk in the front door after school, the atmosphere was felt like molasses, solid enough to cut with a knife.

Mother had reached her only goal—to build a new house. That accomplished, she once again didn't know what to do.

Our house on Barberry Lane was in a cul-de-sac with a circular drive. (It's still there, but since I'm not, past tense seems appropriate.) Like the other five houses in the new subdivision called "Indian Bayou Acres," the Memphis architect designed it with its front facing the bayou. It confused everybody. Built of Roman brick in terra cotta tones bought from the local brick plant, in some ways it might be called mid-century modern; it was low to the ground with dominant horizontal lines, but it was too formal for that description.

The interior was designed by Mother's first cousin, Jim Trice, the son of James Madison Trice, Ganny's brother and only living sibling. Jim was great fun, full of life, and good for Mother. I sometimes wonder if she wanted to build the house so that she could have him around to decorate.

Inside, the décor was elegant and spare (cruel). Silver wallpaper in the foyer. A large fireplace framed in marble and silver in the living room. Above it, an octagonal mirror of Venetian glass. Mother's cousin Jim was partial to Oriental touches, possibly inspired by a large painting Granddaddy Garrard brought Mother from China. The walls were aqua, Mother's favorite color. French doors on both sides of the fireplace led to a wide screened porch facing the bayou, my favorite space. A baby grand piano stood in the corner to the right and beyond it, the library with booklined walls. From the library a long hall led to four bedrooms and three baths. To the left of the living room was a formal dining room. To the left of the entrance was the kitchen and breakfast nook.

In the old neighborhood, Mother and Daddy "drank socially" with their neighbors and friends, but after we moved, Daddy came home every afternoon with a bottle of vodka "hidden" in his zippered jacket. One day after they'd gone out, I was curious to see why the two of them spent so much time in their bathroom, so I snooped. In the cabinet behind the door, I found what looked like a million empty vodka bottles. They must've been waiting to throw them out when the coast was clear.

To compensate for my lack of girls to play with in the new neighborhood, Mother imported a playmate for me from across town. "Julie" was in town with her mother to visit her grandparents.

I'd never met her. She was two or three years younger than me. When she arrived, I expected Mother to help break the ice. In the past, whenever I had friends over to play with, Mother would go to the door with me to greet them and suggest things to do. This time she didn't. When Julie's mother dropped her off, Mother didn't get off the sofa.

Not wanting Julie to see my mother lying there, I took her to the garage and showed her the outdoor storage room that I'd made into a playhouse. I got out my favorite dolls. I was trying to find words to pretend they were talking when I burst into tears. I couldn't stop crying. Julie begged me to tell her what was wrong, but I didn't know. All I knew was that something was wrong with Mother, and I didn't want to tell her that. When I kept crying, Julie got scared and called her mother to come get her. When Julie's mother arrived, she held me by the shoulders and asked me to tell her what was wrong, making me cry harder. I couldn't tell her either.

A week or two later, Julie invited me to her birthday party at her grandparents' house. When she saw me arrive, she ran across the yard to greet me and blurted that she'd *made* her mother invite me. I was mortified and ashamed.

What was wrong with Mother?

Betty Friedan called it the problem with no name. No wonder I couldn't explain it to Julie or her mother. But Betty Friedan and the women's movement that followed were too late for Mother. When she rebelled against the rigid roles for women in Ganny's generation, she lost her footing and had no role to follow.

I found an article in *Wikipedia* (no longer available) by an unnamed author who recreates a conversation between two writers of my mother's generation, Hubert Creekmore and Eudora Welty. The author says that Creekmore thought women hindered themselves by trying to be what they believed men wanted. But Welty believed that male dominance played a bigger part. If these two brilliant writers couldn't agree on where to put the blame, it's no wonder that Mother couldn't. To my mind, the culture blamed the woman, and she in turn blamed herself.

But where did that leave me?

Carl Jung said that the greatest burden a child must carry is a parent's unlived life.[1]

Chapter 19

How Did She Do It?

Ganny and I never talked about my parents' heavy drinking. I knew how I felt, lonely and sad, but only later did I wonder how she felt, how she coped. Though Ganny's bedroom was next to mine in my youth, adolescence, and early adulthood, and I am grateful more than I can say that she was there, I don't feel like I really knew her.

When I learned that Ganny came to live with us at Daddy's invitation, I wondered what Mother said about it. What her feelings were. Was she wary? Was Ganny? Did they worry about the known difficulties between a mother and daughter living in the same household? Did Ganny have any hints of addictive behavior in my mother and daddy before she moved in? Did losing her own mother Anna in any way influence her decision?

Since she didn't tell me, and I didn't ask, I don't know the answers to any of these questions. Our silence was partly temperament. Neither of us was good at expressing our feelings. I know I often discounted mine, while she was trained by her mother or the culture to suppress hers. Her silence may have been an attempt to protect me. I may have been waiting for her to speak first.

We didn't know then that our silence was the norm for most families in the 1950s and strictly enforced in alcoholic families, an unspoken collusion between the non-alcoholic and the alcoholic to keep her (or his) problem a secret so that she can go on drinking. Collusion and silence keep family members from taking steps to

Ganny at Rosemary, Christmas 1956

solve the problem. But Ganny and I knew none of this. We knew little about alcoholism or addiction or how it affects every member of a family.

If she hadn't moved in with Mother and Daddy, what would she have done? I don't think she saw much choice. She'd never lived alone and probably ruled that out on those grounds. She wouldn't have felt comfortable moving in with one of her sons and risk intruding on a daughter-in-law. Living in Mother's house was the most logical answer. When she bought a plot in the Indianola cemetery after Gandaddy died, her purchase indicated she meant to stay.

Raised to be useful, she probably wanted to help with the new baby (me) and help tend my sister Mary, a precocious, endearing eight-year-old. Our modest and unpretentious house in a middle-class neighborhood would have appealed to her.

But it could not have been easy to give up the independence of living in her own home. Though hers was a patriarchal marriage, she had achieved a certain independence by having her own income, working as a music teacher, a bookkeeper, and later managing (owning?) a women's clothing store. She had to accept that she would be dependent on my parents financially, with only her modest widow's pension, and socially, for she didn't drive.

As I've said, Ganny's place on Sunflower Avenue and later Barberry Lane was peripheral; in both houses, her room was at the back. She hid her talents and abilities, fearing perhaps that they would threaten Mother. Ganny was an accomplished cook; Mother never really tried to cook. Ganny joined us only for meals, to fix us treats, to occasionally play the piano, or when we invited her. Otherwise, she stayed in her room. She walked quietly, talked quietly, and entertained herself quietly. For thirty years she kept herself out of the way.

She coped but she didn't thrive. She had friends, mostly bridge-playing ladies her age. On occasion, they'd *gamble* at a *casino* outside the city limits, which sounds more risqué than it was, for the owner, Miss Ina May, ruled over her establishment like she did the Episcopal Church, with an iron, if gloved, hand. (Under her rule, the Episcopal guild ladies were commanded to provide only white wine for communion because red might stain *her* snowy white linens.)

At home Ganny coped, I guess, by being self-entertaining. She spent whole afternoons reading letters from her sons, all regular correspondents. In the secretary, I found hundreds of letters from Cannon to Ganny from all over the world: Persia, Italy, Mexico, England, and many other places. He was always vague about his work, but we had good reason to suspect he worked for the C.I.A. An excellent writer, his letters are treasures that deserve publication. His eyes missed nothing, and his descriptions were vivid. Through letters he and Ganny discussed books they'd read; Jane Austen, Mrs.

Gaskell, and their favorite, Anthony Trollope, probably because he created communities like the one they'd known in Tupelo. In nearly every letter he asks if she needs another Trollope book. Before he died, he'd bought her the whole collection. In their letters back and forth, Ganny and Cannon chatted about Trollope's characters and gossiped about them as if they were friends from Tupelo. Perhaps they liked Jane Austen's communities for the same reason.

In a letter missing its envelope, Cannon writes:

> Which one of Jane Austen's books do you like best? I had a funny experience—read them all like you did & of course started with Pride and Prejudice. I didn't even know about the others. I liked it so much that I read Persuasion & decided I liked it better than the other. Then read Northanger Abbey & liked it better than Persuasion. Then Mansfield Park and when I got to thinking better than N. Abbey I realized that they are all so equal to my taste that which ever one I might be reading would always seem the best. Anyway, Catherine Morland in N. Abbey is my favorite of all heroines . . . Nothing monumentally dramatic or tragic could happen to her as with "regular" heroines because when it tried she just got hungry and ate, then tired, and slept. She couldn't speak well enough to be unintelligible, so she couldn't swap clever talk in the conversational manner of the day. [See Addendum D for another example of Cannon's letters.]

Ganny had other diversions as well. She traveled frequently, always by bus, to see her kin in Shreveport, Louisiana; Camp LeJeune, North Carolina; Charlottesville, Virginia; Chattanooga, Tennessee; and Tupelo, Mississippi. Cannon often offered to pay for her to come see him when he was living in Europe, but she never took him up on it. My cousin Gail (John's daughter) and

I accompanied Ganny on one of her trips to Chattanooga and giggled most of the way because Ganny kept falling asleep, her head lolling over the chair arm as she snored!

Although traveling by bus wasn't easy, she never complained. She made funny stories out of any difficulties. On one trip, she had eggs for breakfast before getting on the bus to Chattanooga. When the driver stopped for lunch at a diner, she only had time to grab an egg sandwich. When she arrived, her daughter-in-law Mary Eleanor greeted her with the news that she'd fixed Ganny "some good old eggs for supper." It may have been the closest Ganny came to complaining.

But her lack of complaint didn't mean she was content. In going through the letters, I almost bypassed an important one because the return address was nearly illegible. When I studied it with a magnifying glass, I nearly fainted. It was from Dr. Eugene B. Elder. Dr. Elder! Eugene! The man she was in love with at Indian Springs!

The letter was written on stationery from the Flagler Hospital, St. Augustine, Florida, and dated December 1, 1946. Both the salutation and closing are handwritten; the rest of the letter is typed. Here are the first and second paragraphs of his five-paragraph letter:

> Do I remember you? Yes, Little Finger, Big 6 remembers the days at Indian Springs, the evening we walked to the Post Office arm in arm, the Organ Grinders serenade, and many other things years ago.
>
> I have traveled over the world and happily married, but no children. I will again retire after war is officially declared over by Congress.

Ganny had obviously written him first. I'd love to know how she found his address. I wish I knew why she wrote to him, and why she wrote him when she did. Was it because she was lonely after losing her husband? Or did his death give her license to look up her old flame? Was the letter just a friendly hello or did she want to know if he was free to rekindle their romance?

I'll never know. But it supports my belief about two things. She was not content in the life she lived on Barberry Lane, and it was a cruel contrast to her stay at Indian Springs. A time when she blossomed. A time when she discovered an autonomous and authentic self. A self in love with life. A self she had to submerge.

Chapter 20

Reprieve

She was a short stout middle-aged lady with dark skin. I liked her immediately. When I was in second grade, she came to cook for us and iron our clothes.

Annie Chapman Collins was wise, kind, and cheerful. Although Mother was her boss and kept a distance, she and Ganny were friends with plenty to talk about: cooking, sewing, and what was going on around town.

Annie was reserved and polite until she saw something that tickled her: a stray cat poking its head in the back door, a pair of mismatched socks, or finding the morning paper in the bushes. Then she'd let out a surprised chortle, bend over double, and let out a laugh that shook her whole body. A laugh to love.

I wish I knew more about her past. I know that her grandparents raised her, that her grandfather worked for the railroad, that she rode with him some of the time, and that they moved around a lot. In her twenties, Annie married Ephraim Collins. They had no children. A few years into their marriage, Ephraim moved to Chicago to open a restaurant and assumed Annie would join him. She went up there with plans to stay, but after a few months, she'd had enough of the brutal winters and came back home. Ephraim came to see her every summer, often driving a nice secondhand car he'd bought for her.

Unlike our previous cooks, Annie didn't mind having me underfoot. I spent a lot of time in the kitchen "helping." I must have had a sixth sense that told me when she was about to make biscuits. Before she could get out the rolling pin, I was in the kitchen, hollering, “Annie! Lemme cut out the biscuits!” I’d pull a stool over to the counter and climb up. After she’d rolled out the dough, she’d hand me the little round top to the blue glass jar that was just the right size.

She was shrewd and streetwise. Sometimes she’d get a wary look while sizing up a situation that was potential trouble. Most Fridays when I was in junior high, six or seven of my friends came over to spend the night. The next morning we’d wake up late and straggle into the kitchen one by one, wanting breakfast. When the last of us had finished eating, it was close to noon and past time for Annie to start the noonday meal. She let our inconsideration go on a few times before putting a stop to it. Next time, she told us, if we straggled into the kitchen one at a time, we’d find it closed. When next time arrived, we got up early, not about to miss her bacon, toast, grits, and fried eggs with crispy edges.

Once I asked Annie to go with me to hear B.B. King sing at his annual Indianola concert. “Humph,” she muttered. “Why would I do that? I grew up hearing B.B. singing over in the next field.” When the B.B. King Museum opened in 2008, I asked her to go with me to see it. After we got there, she turned away from the bleak images of Black people picking cotton, Black people jailed, Black people unemployed and sitting on porches. With her back to the photographs, she started an unrelated conversation.

I was taking notice.

Despite the limitations of being a Black woman in twentieth century Mississippi, Annie took in what she wanted to take in, did what she wanted to do, and taught some silly adolescent girls how to respect her. Although ours was not a mother/daughter relationship, she modeled for me what healthy boundaries looked like. What an empowered woman looked like.

Chapter 21

Scribbles on Scraps

Annie came to work before seven and went home in the early afternoon. After she went home, Ganny closed her door to read or take a nap, and Mary had her own life. With Mother on the sofa watching her soaps, I had to find another source of entertainment. One summer when I was around ten, I decided to write a play. Or tell a play, since I didn't write anything down. After it was finished, I announced to the family that I would be putting on a play in the living room at 11:00 a.m. before dinner (lunch). I remember only one line and only because Mary still repeats it to tease me: "Are the flowers in good health?" one of my lady characters says to another.

After my short stint as a playwright, my writing career languished until the day when Poo, Joy, and I decided to start a column for the town's weekly newspaper. We named it "Teen Tatler" and reported on significant topics such as who was going with whom, who had broken up with whom, and which of the latest fashions was cooler, the chemise dress or the sack. We contributed three columns before the others lost interest. I didn't. It was my first taste of collaboration on a writing project, and I loved it.

It was a busy time for me. On Saturdays, my friends and I would walk wherever we wanted to go—to town and back or along the railroad tracks. We'd walk along the edge of the bayou, and once, when it froze, Poo talked me into skating on it and I fell in. We'd watch "Howdy Doody" and "The Mickey Mouse Club" on television. Joy's parents took us horseback riding and water skiing. But amid these good times, part of me was keeping track of my parents' drinking, and it was getting worse.

After meeting my buddies at the picture show one night, their parents came to pick them up as soon as the movie was over, but mine never came. Mrs. Campbell, a lady I barely knew, saw me waiting and offered me a ride home. I accepted her offer but was so embarrassed that my parents had forgotten me I could hardly speak.

Most nights, when Daddy had too much to drink, he did us all a favor by passing out. It was only a problem when he "fell asleep" in public. One evening after the guests had departed from a party at our house, Daddy was still up and reasonably sober, and I saw an opportunity I might not have again: I tried to talk to him about his drinking. I don't remember what I said, but I remember his reply all too well. "And a little child shall lead them," he said. The tears filling his eyes gave me hope.

One night after another party when the guests had left, an uncle stayed behind to talk to Mother and Daddy about their drinking. Daddy must have guessed what was coming because he slipped out of the room. Mother kept a firm arm around me. My uncle pointedly looked at me said, "I think it's time for someone to tippy off to bed." Bristling at his interference, Mother tightened her hold on me.

But my uncle's advice to Mother on sobriety didn't take. Her moods worsened. She was touchy and unpredictable. Her sense of entitlement grew stronger. She yelled at the butcher in the grocery store, she yelled at Daddy for snoring, she yelled at me for putting my books down in her perfect living room when I came home from school instead of taking them to my room. Although she encouraged me to invite friends over to spend the night, she would yell at me if we woke her up.

In a mother-daughter relationship already fraught with problems, alcohol made it an inferno. Mother must have seen herself in me, the daughter most like her. We looked alike, both petite, both blue-eyed with light brown hair, both had noses with character. We both loved to read. We were both sensitive, sometimes clueless, and sometimes flustered. She didn't cook, and although I've done my share of cooking, it's not my long suit. Even as Mother withdrew from me emotionally, she tried to live *through* me. Hers was a possessive love with long-lasting ramifications.

If we hadn't once been close, her withdrawal wouldn't have cut so deeply. It wasn't about her rages, though they were plenty scary and embarrassing. It wasn't about her unpredictability: one minute she thought I was the cutest person in the world—I *was* her world—and the next, I was the enemy trying to come between her and her vodka. It was about what she was doing to herself, and the trauma in watching her do it.

When my hurt became too complicated to contain, I flattened her into the Bad Mother and told myself only the stories to confirm this view. I hated her. Hated what she'd become. Hated what she'd destroyed. Hated her looks: drinking had thickened her waist and misshaped her once lovely figure. She was no longer "teeny." Her face was red from drink and rosacea.

My strategy, mostly unconscious, was to show her how wrong she was by going to Sunday School, church, and Training Union at the Baptist Church. She and Daddy were not churchgoers, and I was sure that was the problem. I became an earnest little Christian. Every few weeks there was an altar call, and the preacher invited (implored, begged) us to "come on down," confess our sins, and rededicate our lives. After about twenty repetitions of "Just as I Am" from the choir and more pleadings from the preacher, my friend and I would hang our heads and trudge to the altar to admit our nonexistent sins. What was this about? On one level, it didn't make sense. But on another, it did. We were two sad girls who had problems too big to solve, and so we turned to a minister who promised relief. Years later, a former schoolmate and member of the same church told me that his only prayer in those days was for the Almighty to please not let those girls rededicate their lives again, prolonging his misery.

In 1959, Cannon died unexpectedly in a hotel in Mexico at age fifty-two. One morning soon after his death, Mother was lying in bed later than usual. Seeing her grim look and hoping to cheer her up, I offered her some religious platitude, maybe something about Cannon being with Jesus now. Mother glared at me and brusquely dismissed my words. "At your age, I wanted to be a missionary," she spat out bitterly, implying many things. Among them, the idea that I would or should outgrow such piety.

Though I may have been wrongheaded in trying to help her find salvation, I wasn't completely wrong and despite her contempt, I've never lost my sense of a Presence. In *Alcoholics Anonymous (the big book)*, Bill W. says that he could not have gotten sober without the sense of a higher power, and his insight became the foundation of A.A.

In desperation, I began to scribble notes on scraps of paper of what I'd seen and how I felt. I rolled them up and hid them in a hollow clothes rod in my closet. As with many co-dependents, *my* secret was their alcoholism. (For all I know, the notes are still there.) The scraps of paper, paltry as they were, became a step out of silence. A tiny beginning that showed me the power of writing, how it could transmute pain and help me develop a sense of identity apart from my parents. My next step was to write to Mary, then at Harvard, and tell her how difficult life had become on Barberry Lane. I pleaded with her to tell me what to do. She wrote me sweet, consoling letters that I immediately threw away, afraid that Mother or Daddy would see them.

Chapter 22

Accident?

The body keeps the score and finds a way to tell it.

I am in ninth grade. It's Friday night after a football game. Six of my girlfriends and I are walking to Andrea's house to pick up her pajamas before walking to my house for a spend-the-night party. We're fourteen, not quite old enough for a driver's license, so when Ed, a year older and licensed, offers us a ride, it is welcome. Three of the others climb into his two-door car. Joy, Kathryn, and I hop on the hood. I am sitting on the driver's side, unaware that I am blocking Ed's view. Moments later, the car crashes into a car parked on the side of a quiet residential street, and my left leg is pinned between them. Kathryn and Joy are thrown onto the street and suffer minor scrapes and bruises.

My scream wakes up everyone in the neighborhood. They come running out of their houses. One of them is the sheriff, who calls an ambulance and tries to keep me still until it arrives. I am rushed to the local hospital. My leg is a bloody mess, and x-rays will soon show that I have multiple fractures.

I am on a gurney in the operating room under the glare of fluorescent lights. The doctor on call is smoking a cigar as he examines my leg and tries to decide what to do. Mother and Daddy rush in. "Put out that damn cigar," Mother yells. "You are spilling ashes all over her."

I don't realize how serious my injuries are until I see the tears in my parents' eyes and the alarm in their faces. They hold onto me. For a long time, nothing seems to happen. Then the doctor calls them out of the room, and after what seems a long time, they come back to tell me that the doctor has decided to send me to Campbell's Clinic in Memphis, one of the best orthopedic clinics in the South. "No," I yell. "I'm NOT going."

• • •

At Campbell's Clinic, the doctors operated and then put my leg in traction for two months—a lifetime to me at fourteen. Mother checked into the guest wing of the hospital, and except for one weekend, she stayed with me the entire time even though I had nurses round the clock.

Mother and I watched "I Love Lucy" every day. We ate candy and gossiped about people back home. She changed the water in my vases of get-well flowers. Mother took her only break when Dr. Millford came in to play a daily game of checkers with me, a respite from his rounds that astonished and flattered me to pieces. He seemed to enjoy our games as much as I did and seemed annoyed if he was paged. I discovered that I was a pretty good player, good enough anyway to give him a challenge. When Mother decided to go home for that one weekend, I selfishly begged her not to go.

There is no doubt in my mind that my "accident" was an unconscious cry for help. And it worked. I got my mother back, I got my Daddy back, and I got the attention from each of them that I hadn't had in a long time. Even when I was released from the hospital in a body cast that immobilized me for two more months, Mother and Daddy continued to be kind, caring, and kept their drinking under control. Mother was pleasant even when emptying my bedpan and making me sandwiches. She had a purpose.

Ganny insisted on visiting one of her sons and that my hospital bed be placed in her room so that I could enjoy her big picture window. Or at least that was the reason she gave. Likely, she noticed the renewed attention Mother and Daddy were giving me and stepped out of the way.

Daddy's response to my accident was to buy me a new car even though I was still six months away from getting my license. It made sense to him. If he'd been in my place, a new car would have made him happy—he loved cars—and he must have hoped it would do the same for me. It did.

Mother was furious. She thought it was crazy to reward me with a *car* after my leg had been crushed by one. But it gave me something to look forward to and made the time go faster. He drove my new car to Memphis every weekend (except for that one when Mother went home) and parked it so that I could see it from my bed. It was a 1960 Chevrolet Impala convertible, white with a red interior and a red stripe down the side—the coolest car I (and my friends) had ever seen.

Sometimes Daddy came on a day trip so that he could bring my friends. He was a great sport, and they adored him. He'd let them play anything they wanted on the radio and tease them later about their awful music: "Seven Little Girls Sitting in the Back Seat" (huggin' and a kissin' with Fred), "The Purple People-eater," "Itsy Bitsy Teeny Weeny Yellow Polka Dot Bikini," and "Charlie Brown" with its deep-voice refrain "Why's Everybody Always Picking on Me?"

When I was finally freed from my body cast, my friends and I had some great times in my convertible, both before and after I got my license. The town gossips didn't like it and thought we were wild. We knew what they were saying because Ann's mother, Ruth, owned a beauty shop and told us. But she said not to pay them any attention. Ruth always thought the best of us even when we were being somewhat irresponsible. We wasted a lot of time, money, and gas riding around and wasted even more by riding around in winter with the top down and the heater going full blast. But, otherwise, we had no sins to confess.

After I recovered, Mother and Daddy resumed their heavy drinking. They had given me everything except the one thing I wanted—their sobriety.

One summer afternoon, my friends and I were on the screened porch, laughing and cutting up. Mother came out and spoke to me sharply about something I no longer remember. I called her a bitch *in front of my friends*. Looking like she'd been slapped, she turned and and left in a huff.

Later, as I was leaving the house in my car, I was about to pass Mother and Daddy coming in. Daddy flagged me down. With a look of disappointment on his face I had never seen and a sternness in his voice I'd never heard, he told me to apologize to my mother. Even though she was on the far side of the front seat, I could see all too well her injured eyes. I *was* sorry that I'd hurt her and meant it when I apologized. But I knew that her hurt feelings shouldn't have been the main issue. I needed discipline.

I was more careful around my mother after that. My hostility went underground.

Chapter 23

Cathedral Days

I missed five months of my ninth-grade year because of my broken leg, but my teachers passed me on to tenth grade. Concerned about my education and remembering the forlorn letters I'd written, Mary came up with the idea of my going to boarding school. She suggested National Cathedral School for Girls in Washington, D.C., where Mabelle and Mary Jayne had gone a generation earlier. Mary would be nearby. Having recently received her PhD from Johns Hopkins University, she was now a professor at American University in D.C.

When Mother and Daddy took her suggestion seriously, I was furious—furious at Mother and Daddy for *not* parenting me and at Mary for playing what should have been their role. That year of sad letters was *then*. This was *now*: I was happy with my friends and didn't want to leave.

Having abdicated, Mother and Daddy left the decision up to me. It felt like they didn't care what I decided, but maybe they were as conflicted as I was.

I loved my girlfriends and had recently discovered boys. I didn't want to be dragged away just when things were going so well. And besides, if I went away, I would no longer be able to drive my beautiful Impala convertible with the red stripe down the side.

Not knowing what else to do, I asked my friends to help me throw a party. (It was a Delta thing—when in doubt, throw a party.) After talking six friends into co-hosting it (it wasn't hard), we decided that we'd have a luau, the most exotic idea we could think of, that we'd pay for it ourselves, and that we'd invite the *boys*.

We mowed lawns. We transformed my screened porch by taking off the legs of the ping pong table and lowering it to the floor. We removed cushions from all the chairs and put them around the table. Though it looked more like a Roman banquet than a luau, to our eyes it was perfect. We bought watermelons, cantaloupes, and honeydew melons, and cut them into cubes. The boys came and showed their appreciation by busting a watermelon on the porch steps and leaving shards all over the lawn.

Whatever. It was a good party because its real success was the deepening bond between my girlfriends and me. We began to open up to each other and share our troubles. Each of us had something big to deal with, alcoholism, overcontrolling parents, indifferent parents, absent parents, or "broken homes" (as we called them back then), but we were no longer alone. On any given day, we knew the safe houses for hanging out and the ones to avoid until the binge or tirade ended. Between us there were two parents we could always count on, Jo's dad, Roy, and Ann's mother, Ruth.

But I still had to decide what to do about school. Ganny left a note on my pillow about the importance of my education and that she didn't want me to ever feel inferior. *Aloquis Excelcius*. The only note I ever got from her, and it wasn't much help.

At the last possible minute, I decided to go. But Cathedral school admissions put a condition on my acceptance. My placement scores showed a deficiency in Latin, due to my five-month absence in ninth grade, and they wanted me to repeat the tenth. I changed my mind again. I would not go. The headmistress stepped in and said if I could learn a year's worth of Latin in the three summer months before school started, she'd place me in the eleventh grade. What? And lose my summer that was supposed to be for luaus and riding around? I agreed to go to Cathedral as a tenth grader and suck up my humiliation.

• • •

Those first months at Cathedral, I was unhappy most of the time. My throat was swollen with homesickness. I missed my mother, but how could that be when I didn't even like her? When my roommate decided to go back home, I wanted to go home too and would have except that it would mean being a grade behind my classmates back home.

One of my biggest heartbreaks was leaving my convertible behind. Daddy solved the problem by giving it to Mary. Maybe he pictured the two of us helling around together with the top down. Truth was we rarely got together. She was busy teaching, and I was only allowed to go out occasionally. How could Daddy give her the car he'd given me? The worst insult came when I discovered that Mary had gone to a repair shop and had the beautiful red stripe painted black. Soooo uncool. I took it personally. It made me feel like she was shaming my lifestyle, shaming me, but with so many unsorted feelings, I never told her. A few months later, she sold the car and bought one she considered less showy, more tasteful.

Dark days. I withdrew into myself, living in my memories: Me and the gang fixing our own flats, ordering spaghetti for breakfast at Labella's, playing touch football in the park with the boys, running out of gas, then buying only a dollar's worth and running out again.

After the freedom I'd had at home, I chafed at the school's rules. We envied the day students who could go home after school. Even the privileges we had were regimented. On Saturdays we could go off campus but only within two blocks of the school. We could go out with friends but only with written permission from home. We got up by a bell, went to classes and study hall by a bell, went to dinner by a bell, and bed by a bell.

When she could, Mary sprang me and took me to lunch or to her apartment for an overnight. In my second year, after my cousin Jamie enrolled, Mary and her friend Diane took us to Harper's Ferry for the weekend. Released from boarding-school jail, Jamie and I were as silly as two adolescent girls could be, and to our surprise, Mary and Diane, both brilliant academics, acted as silly as we did. But those reprieves were rare, and when I returned to the dorm afterwards, I was even more miserable.

Just when things were at their darkest, Mrs. Davis, my tenth-grade English teacher, changed my life. I felt an immediate connection: She was about five feet tall, my height, and her first name was the same as mine though she spelled it Marian with an "a"—but close enough.

Because of my last-minute decision to go to Cathedral, I hadn't read the twelve books on the reading list required for tenth-grade English. Mrs. Davis said she would excuse me if I could read the entire list of books over the next six weeks. I did it, surprising us both. She praised me. She *saw* me. Not the bratty girl I'd been but the one I was becoming.

I loved her classes. When she taught a story by, say, Rumer Godden or Katherine Mansfield, she rose on her toes in excitement. At times she was so eager to answer our questions or explain something, she couldn't get her words out. Years later when I started teaching, my style was very much like hers. I got excited when I could feel a student connect with something we were discussing, and though I don't think I rose on my toes, my speech would falter just like Mrs. Davis's.

She had a deep sense of social justice. At the end of the year, she told us that she was going to resign from Cathedral and teach in the D.C. public schools. Over our howls of protest, she said, "You girls don't need me. You'll learn no matter what. But the kids in public school might not. Please think about that."

In my eleventh-grade year, my history teacher, Mrs. Acheson, was formative too but not in the same way. She awed us all. She was a *writer*. She had published a book! On the Supreme Court! She was tall, slender, and blonde. We were dazzled by her elegance and more dazzled by her complete indifference to what she wore. I remember a green and red plaid kilt and a yellow cardigan over a Villager blouse with a floral print. Fashion forward! When she told us the least thing about herself—that she'd switched to Carlton cigarettes—we were fascinated.

Though she could be condescending and wore a perpetual sneer, we worshipped her anyway as only teenage girls can. She could lecture without notes on any era of American history or politics. She would throw out her pearls of knowledge in an off-handed way as if she was still talking about the merits of Carltons, and if we caught these gems of wisdom, fine. If not, well, too bad.

One day, she swooped into class in one of her mismatched outfits and waved a hand in my direction. I was sitting on the front row, expecting a lecture on the Constitution when she pointed directly at me. Her brown eyes bored into mine and in a haughty voice, she pelted out her words: "Marion! What. Is. Going. On. Down. There?"

I was stunned. Clueless. My face grew hot. Holding back tears, I lowered my eyes and slipped down in my chair. With my heart thudding in my ears, I could only catch her words here and there: *Mississippi. James Meredith. Mississippi. Protest. Riot. Mississippi. National Guard. Wrong. Down there. Mississippi.* It was September 30, 1962, and she had just heard on the news that African American Air Force veteran James Meredith had enrolled at Ole Miss, and a deadly riot had broken out.

I felt like I had somehow failed the entire state of Mississippi and didn't know how to fix it. My shame and guilt hung on for years.

In September of 2022, on the sixtieth anniversary of James Meredith's entry into Ole Miss, Meredith was interviewed by a reporter for the *Clarion-Ledger*. He said that though Mississippians have a long way to go, "I still think Mississippi is going to lead this nation, and the world, to another formula on dealing with the Black-White thing. Ain't nobody thought as much about the Black-White situation than Black and White people in Mississippi."[1]

• • •

It took me a long time to unpack Mrs. Acheson's attack and see it for what it was—unfair, unjustified, and mean. I was a sixteen-year-old student, and she was my teacher with all the authority on her side.

Twenty years later, she called me up but not to apologize, as I wildly thought at first. She had seen in the Cathedral newsletter that I was teaching at Delta State University in Cleveland, Mississippi, and wanted to ask a *favor*. Now that's interesting, I thought.

"There's a marker on your campus," she said.

"The one about your father-in-law, you mean."

She seemed surprised. But how could I not know that in 1947 her father-in-law, Dean Acheson, had delivered his famous speech announcing the Marshall Plan at Delta Council on the Delta State campus.

"Would you take a photo of his historic marker and send it to me?"

"I'd be glad to," I said, sweetly, bygones forgotten. And I did.

• • •

I'd done well in Mrs. Davis's class and continued to do well in English in my junior and senior years. All three of my English teachers encouraged my writing. Miss Nelson, my teacher in the junior year, stopped me after class to praise a critique I'd written.

I was named runner-up for the coveted Hyde Prize, based on a piece of writing we had to produce within a limited, carefully monitored time frame. When the other runner-up and I were summoned to the office of Miss Lee, the headmistress, we thought we were about to be reprimanded for something we'd done and were scared to death. Katherine Lee was an imposing woman with large eyes magnified by glasses that made them look enormous. When speaking to us, she'd look slightly off to the side, so we were never sure if she was speaking to us. As it turned out, she'd summoned us to commend us on our writing, but I was too intimidated to hear her praise.

• • •

Coming from Mississippi, I often felt like I was a different species. Many of my sophisticated classmates, especially the day students, were children of diplomats, ambassadors, rocket scientists (Robert Oppenheimer), or U.S. presidents (Lyndon Johnson). They had seen far more of the world than I had, sheltered as I'd been in the "closed society" of Mississippi.

On Flag Day, celebrated every month in the Cathedral (the church not the school), two girls were chosen to carry their state flag in the Sunday procession. Until my cousin Jamie enrolled, I was the only student from Mississippi. Consequently, on Mississippi's day, I had to carry the flag alone in a long procession to the great altar. Scotland was also being celebrated, and I was lost in a sea of bagpipes, an image that magnificently expresses how I felt that first year.

We boarders lived for going home on holidays, and as they neared, we'd sing our "vacation song" at dinner. "Ten more days till vacation (nine, eight, seven . . .), then we'll go to the station, the plane will carry us there." As we reached the three-day mark, the two-day mark, and then the one-day mark, our excitement mounted, and our voices grew louder.

That first Thanksgiving, Mother and Daddy met my flight in Memphis. But when at Christmas, they sent Mose Wilson, our handyman, to pick me up, I was devastated. I liked Mose. He could not have been kinder to me. But he wasn't a substitute for my parents. On that long drive home from Memphis, I struggled to make conversation because one thought kept intruding: *How could they? How could they?*

Reuniting with my old classmates when I came home was another trial. Boarding school was changing me. I no longer shared the interests of my old friends and vice versa. (Later, I rediscovered these old classmates and joined them for many happy class reunions.) Much of the time, I was homesick at school and lonely at home. As always, Ganny was my refuge. She listened attentively to all my stories about school, my friends, and my studies. But I didn't mention homesickness, and I put my difficulties in the best possible light. I never let on that, despite the hopes she'd expressed in her note to me, boarding school had not diminished my feelings of inferiority. It had increased them.

My Cathedral years were marked by highly significant historical events. When the Bay of Pigs confrontation came to a crisis on April 17, 1961, we boarders were hustled into assembly and warned of imminent danger, but the head of the dormitory explained the situation so abstractly that we felt no sense of impending peril. When President Kennedy was assassinated on November 22, 1963, we all felt the shock, bone deep. We were all allowed to go to the funeral and were bussed downtown. A piercing sadness came over me when the riderless horse passed by. President Kennedy's death felt like a personal loss that I couldn't comprehend.

In our senior year, possibly because the administrators wanted us to leave with good things to say, our restrictions were loosened.

We were allowed to smoke (!) in the clubhouse, and since it was a badge of being a senior, how could we not? We were allowed to go unchaperoned to Georgetown to shop or have lunch. It didn't take us long to find the Rathskeller, where we'd heard that no IDs were required, and we discovered beer.

Exciting as they were, these new privileges didn't compare to an event that occurred in early spring of our senior year. On February 11, 1964, the Beatles gave their first U.S. performance at the Washington Coliseum in D.C., and we were allowed to attend. I didn't faint, but along with the other eight thousand fans, I screamed my lungs out and temporarily impaired my hearing.

While writing this chapter, I got out a yearbook and read some of the inscriptions. Though they were the affectionate notes typical of yearbooks, I realized I had made many close friends. When I went back to Cathedral a few years later, I saw that, though the dorm I stayed in still looked like a stone fortress, the grounds were lovely, the Bishop's Garden was enchanting, and the Cathedral itself was magnificent.

My Cathedral years were full of extremes—intense sadness and intense joy. Who could ask for more?

Chapter 24

New Orleans (by way of Columbia, Missouri)

Cathedral was reputed to be an excellent preparatory school that promoted the idea that students would get into the college of their choice. But the first two colleges I applied to, Vanderbilt and Newcomb, turned me down.

I took these rejections hard. For most of my life, I'd been compared to my gifted sister who'd attended Newcomb, Harvard, and Johns Hopkins. To their credit, my parents never compared us in any way, but while I was still in elementary school, a friend of theirs pinched my cheek and said, "You're just as smart as Mary." Until that moment, I hadn't given it a thought.

Mother wouldn't have compared me anyway, because she had other plans for me. Since Mary was the smart one, I was to be the social one. As described in several letters Mother wrote to Mary in 1964–1965 (and she saved for me), my role was clear. The first letter was written in the summer of 1964. By that time, I'd made a second round of applications to Southern Methodist University and Stephens College and been accepted at both. An administrator in the Newcomb admissions office told me that if I made my grades my freshman year, I *might* be accepted as a transfer in my sophomore year. I decided to go to Stephens, make my grades, and transfer to Newcomb. I don't know why I'd become obsessed with going to Newcomb. I don't know if I was trying to be "just as smart as Mary" (impossible) or because I wanted to go where Mother and Mary had both gone.

In the first letter, Mother says how tired she is of the Democratic convention and of seeing Luci Baines Johnson's hair "blotting out the screen." (She and Daddy were for Goldwater.) But the focus of the letter is my upcoming debutante party. Stapled to the letter is an invitation to the other debs to come to a champagne supper at "Woodlawn" (the first I knew of our house having a name) on September 1, 1964, at 10 o'clock in the evening. The guest singer would be Miss Mary Rinehart, an Indianola neighbor and friend.

Mother says, "I am now trying to compete with the Equen Plantation party, which is impossible . . . Mike said it was sure to be written up in the *New York Times*." (Mike was my date, who would become a lifelong friend.)

Though the party wasn't written up in the *New York Times*, it was spectacular. Held on the grounds of Equen Plantation a few miles outside of Greenwood, it might have been Hollywood. Mike and I could see it miles away on the country road leading to it. The whole place was lit up with hundreds of Japanese lanterns hanging from what looked like thousands of live oaks. On our arrival, servants appeared in white coats to offer exotic hors d'oeuvres and flutes of champagne. Bands played from three different pavilions built for dancing.

In her letter, Mother describes the plans for our party. "Ours will be ours & they'd damn well better have a good time." She tells Mary she hopes she'll come and that Ganny has offered to pay her expenses. I could picture Mary's reaction. Though she too had made her debut, her career was demanding; there were books to read, books and articles to write, classes and seminars to attend. A debut party, even mine, would have been the farthest thing from her mind.

The parties were fun, but I saw even then that being a debutante was about elitism, exclusivity, class, heritage, wealth, and *Whiteness*. It was a charade that would never give me a sense of the belonging I craved. Beneath the frilly dress of the debutante was a serious girl who needed direction, who needed *meaning*.

About a year ago I had a dream that I was making my debut. I shared it with the Dream Group I've belonged to for over twenty years. A few days later, Chrissy, one of the members, brought me a tee shirt to honor the dream. Across the front, the message says: "Jesus Don't Care if You a Debutante." I loved it! At first, I took it to mean that Jesus would overlook my decision to make my debut. Then I learned the backstory online. The designer of the tee shirt said he'd overheard a teenage Black girl saying the words to a friend and intended it to mean, "Jesus don't care if you [not] a debutante." I laughed out loud when I got the second meaning and saw how I'd taken it all so seriously. *Get over yourself, White girl.*

In the fall, I went to Stephens College in Columbia, Missouri. In a letter dated October 9, 1964, after I'd been at Stephens a month, Mother sent Mary the entire six-week report from my advisor who said:

> Marion's adjustment to class work has been very good. She is eager to learn & willing to work hard at it. Her study program is nicely balanced and, I think, right for her. Outside of class she is unusually poised, articulate, and sensitive. What adjustment problems she is having stem from her maturity. She knows what she wants and is not yet certain that she is finding it. I have no doubt that the picture will be clearer for her after a term here.

A kind report, warmer than those sent from Cathedral. But I dismissed the praise. *Mature.* Well, yeah. But that was because I was a year older than most of the students and had already attended a girls' school. *I knew what I wanted.* Not in the larger sense, but I knew I wanted to go to Newcomb. *Eager to learn, classwork good.* I was motivated to make good grades but only so that I could transfer to Newcomb. *Poised, articulate, sensitive.* I didn't feel poised or articulate. Only sensitive seemed to apply. Mother made no comment to me about the report. Instead, she deferred to Mary, saying, "Write us your comments when you have time."

Even though Stephens was a means to an end, it was a good choice. I was happy there. My roommate, Caron, was from Gulfport, Mississippi, and we had a lot in common. We were close and traveled to England and Scotland together after we left Stephens. We made friends with three other girls on our floor, and the five of us became inseparable.

When Caron's mother came to visit her, I saw what a healthy mother-daughter relationship looked like. When Mrs. Waller entered our dorm room and saw Caron, she let out a whoop of sheer joy. No secrets, no eggshells, no strings, or hidden agendas. Just joy.

At the end of the year, I reapplied to Newcomb and was accepted. On September 9, 1965, I was on my way to New Orleans to register at Newcomb when I turned on the car radio. Hurricane Betsy was aimed directly at New Orleans.

I stopped at a service station and called Aunt Marion and Uncle Jimmy Rives with whom I'd planned to spend the first night (just as Daddy had thirty years before). Uncle Jimmy answered and said, "If you want to attend Newcomb this semester, you'd better come on." When I reached New Orleans, the palm trees were swaying unnaturally. Some of their fronds touched the ground. It would soon become a Category Four hurricane.

I was so scared that I forgot the directions to the Rives's uptown house on Jefferson Street. Impulsively, I hailed a cab, gave the driver the address, and followed him.

We stayed up all night listening to the storm. After it abated, we went around the premises to check on everything. Except for shattered panes in an upstairs bay window and debris in the yard, all was well. Like the palms, the two-story wood-frame house knew how to sway and bend in the wind. Thousands were not so lucky.

On opening day, I was one of only a handful of girls to arrive at Newcomb. Most students had stayed home to wait out the storm and its aftermath, but later I was glad I hadn't. When I heard that classes had been suspended for a week, I saw it as an opportunity to do whatever I wanted. I called my first cousin, David Clark, John's son, who was attending a branch of LSU in New Orleans and asked him to come see me. He sounded happy to hear from me.

With David, I felt an instant rapport and before the week was out, we'd declared ourselves soulmates. Having lost his mother, Bessie, when he was twelve, he was kind, sensitive, and wiser than his twenty years. I wondered if our affinity was because of our strong family resemblance, or because we were both Pisces, or if it was because we had Ganny to talk about if the conversation lagged, though it never did.

At night, when the heat was almost bearable, we'd walk around his neighborhood near Carrollton Avenue, where he lived in a house with his maternal grandmother while attending LSU. We'd stop and look up at the stars and talk. We talked about infinity, eternity, death, and God. We contemplated why we were here and wondered what we should do with our lives. Though we would never again live in the same city, we became lifelong friends. In a life that ended too soon from Parkinson's disease and other major health issues, he never lost his sense of wonder—or humor. Over the years our close relationship continued by long conversations on the phone. Before we hung up, one of us would always say, "Goodbye, soulmate." Only weeks before he died, he sent me a book by Richard Rohr from St. Dominic's Resting Home in Houston.

Recently, David's sister Gail told me that her father, John, had been an alcoholic, which I'd suspected, and that David had been too, which I never knew. This information partially explained my immediate feeling of closeness to David. I had a radar for an alcoholic or child of an alcoholic, and he'd been both. Like my children, David got help and stopped drinking in young adulthood. Gail said that after he conquered his addiction, he became an inspiration to a lot of people in the Houston area struggling with their addictions and founded a support group.

• • •

Soon after classes started, I met with my academic advisor who said my grades and SAT scores should have been satisfactory for admission and wondered aloud why I hadn't been accepted when I first applied. After the circuitous route I'd taken to get there, I could only stare at her in disbelief.

Having finally arrived, I didn't know who I was or what I was supposed to do. At Cathedral, I'd had a goal of staying the course for three years. At Stephens, my goal was to get into Newcomb. Now I floundered. The teachers seemed lackluster, but maybe it was me. I wasn't interested in any of my classes except literature and writing. My parents didn't care about my grades. They had Mary for showing their smart genes. They had me for . . . what? I didn't know.

I took a creative writing class under a professor who established no ground rules for student critiquing, nothing about saying something kind, or how to constructively criticize. Instead of asking us read our stories aloud, he read them to us himself, and it was easy enough to detect a scornful tone when he didn't like something.

In one of my stories, I made up the plot and circumstances but used the real names of people in Indianola since no one in the class would know them. I used catchy names like Georgia Gresham and

Virginia Van Cleve. But after Dr. M. read my story to the group, one of the guys in the circle shook his head and said, "The names, man. They're unreal." Overcoming my embarrassment, I saw his point and had to laugh.

My American literature professor was so shy he could barely look up from his notes. He read them to us word for word in a monotone. Once in the middle of reading his notes to us, he said something about "Emerson's underlying theory of the universe" and then moved on to his next sentence. By that time, all of us were comatose—all except my roommate, Martha, who raised her hand and said, "Excuse me, sir, but what was Emerson's underlying theory of the universe?" Dr. P. blushed and chuckled, whether at her alertness or at his own obtuseness, I'm not sure. He cleared his throat. "Unity-in-variety," he answered drily with a nod in her direction.

If I was underwhelmed by Dr. M. and Dr. P., when I took a course on southern writers, I woke up. There I discovered Walker Percy. I identified with characters like the lost, alienated Binx Bolling in *The Moviegoer* and recognized myself in his search for authenticity. But when I was introduced to Will Barrett in *The Last Gentlemen*, an amnesiac southerner living in New York, who works as a janitor but calls himself an engineer, I adored him for being as confused and estranged as I was.

One scene in *The Last Gentleman* blew me away. When Barrett goes on a road trip to chase a woman he's fallen in love with, he winds up in Ithaca, Mississippi, a thinly disguised Greenville. (Percy establishes that it is Greenville by references to a tamale vendor, a "Chinaman's store," and a cottonseed mill.) Barrett searches for the house he grew up in and when he finds it, his amnesia falls away. He reimagines and remembers the scene of his father's suicide. When I read the passage, something resonated deeply. Though Barrett's childhood trauma was nothing like mine, for the first time I saw the connection between my parents' addictions and my floundering.

Chapter 25

Why Did She Stay?

While I was off at school, I often wondered and worried about Ganny and how she was coping.

Among her books—Austen, Gaskell, and Trollope—I discovered one a few years ago called *Peace of Mind* by Rabbi Joshua Liebman, published in 1946. On the flyleaf, Ganny inscribed in ink her name and the date, May May Clark, 1947, which was two years after her husband's death and two years after she moved in with us. It suggests to me that she was never as content as she pretended to be.

Peace of Mind is still in print. It combines the most advanced, enlightened views of religion at the time with the psychology of Freud and his successors, one of the first to do so. When I read it with Ganny in mind, one sentence jumped out at me: "The technique of repression—the tight-lipped denial of all our hostile and sensual thoughts—simply has not worked!"[1]

Sometimes, when I was with Ganny, she'd get a stricken look, put a hand to her forehead, and seem to stop breathing. When asked what was wrong, she'd lift a shoulder in a helpless shrug and wait for it to pass. What *could* she say? That she was here at the generosity of her daughter and son-in-law, but they made her want to cry?

Why didn't Ganny leave? From what I have learned from Mary, there was a time when she almost did. I was at boarding school, so I don't know the details, but one night while drinking more heavily than usual, either Mother or Daddy accidentally locked Ganny out of the house before going to bed. I don't know how long she was locked out or how she got back in, but she later broke down and told her son Saville about it. For her to break out of her long-held reserve and tell Saville meant the event was enormously disturbing. Mary remembers that Saville tried to get her to move in with him and Renie in Charlottesville, but she wouldn't do it.

• • •

About the time Ganny started writing her memoirs, she began having heart trouble. When she saw our family doctor, he diagnosed her with angina.

In *Swamplands of the Soul*, James Hollis says, "The etymological root of the words *anger*, *angst*, *anxiety*, and *angina* comes from the Indo-Germanic *angh*, which means 'to constrict.'" He explains that the root of the word shows the relationship between angst and angina; angst is restricted emotion, and angina is the restricted flow of blood through the veins. He continues: "Yet for many, anger was not tolerated in the family circle. Thus, when the child felt the wounding of psychic 'constriction,' the unacceptable emotional response was channeled into acting out, repression as depression, or widening a shadow split within."[2]

In 1959, Cannon died of a heart attack alone in a motel room in Mexico. He was only fifty-three. He died without ever letting on who employed him, though we have reason to believe it was the CIA. If he told Ganny, she kept it a secret like so much else. She would have deeply grieved his death, but she never showed her anguish to me.

In her last years, Ganny suffered extremely painful angina attacks, usually in the middle of the night. She never cried out in pain, but she would let Mother know, and Mother would call the doctor who lived only a few houses away and, for Ganny, he made house calls. He would come over immediately and give her a shot of nitroglycerin and after a while her pain abated. I was with her during many of these episodes, saw her in obvious agony but never heard her make a sound.

With all good intentions, the doctor told Ganny to smoke a cigarette every day. He believed that it would improve her circulation; the dangers of cigarettes wouldn't become known until two years later. On a whim that proved wiser than she knew, she bought a filter for her cigarettes, a long, slender black one that I called her "movie-star filter."

Despite the painful angina attacks, her long-suppressed buoyant spirit inexplicably surfaced. She bought herself a pair of sporty red tennis shoes and started listening to the music of Elvis Presley. Though dubious about him at first, when she learned he was a Tupelo boy, she became his biggest fan and went to see him in *Jailhouse Rock*—more than once!

And then she decided to write her memoir. I can still see her sitting in the floral chair with her plywood lapboard across its arms. I see her as she writes, pauses and looks out the window at the Magnolia Frascati. Her pen hovers. Then she continues, blue ink flowing evenly across the page. Thank goodness, she never closed her door.

She died on January 5, 1967. She was buried in the Indianola cemetery next to her husband Robert and her son Cannon. She slipped out of our lives as quietly as she'd slipped in. Born on Christmas day, she died on Twelfth Night, two sacred holidays framing a life well lived.

Chapter 26

Love and Marriage

Two months after Ganny died, I met my future husband. In some ways Claiborne reminds me of her. Like her, he is a sensate who expresses himself through the material world. For her, it was in making teacakes or oyster stew, sewing, and playing the piano. For him, it is in building things, cooking, growing things, and being an all-around "Mr. Fixit." As I once told my friend Dorothy, "He knows how to make a day interesting." She liked the sentence so much she used it in a novel. At seventy-nine, he still knows how to make a day interesting.

He has a Zen intelligence, so unlike the academic kind I'd been chasing. I'm not sure what I mean by "Zen intelligence." To me, it's being grounded, being in the moment, being able to work with whatever is at hand. Unlike my mind, full of abstract ideas and preconceived notions.

Ours is a complementary relationship. Claiborne is good with details whereas I can usually see the big picture. When he first moved to New Orleans, he lived in an apartment with his brother Bobby and a couple of other guys. His room wasn't much bigger than a closet, so he built a bunk bed and planned to sleep on the top and use the bottom as a closet. When I went over to see his progress, I couldn't help but notice he was building it *in the living room.* As diplomatically as I could, I suggested continuing the construction in the bedroom because, otherwise, it wasn't going to fit through the narrow bedroom door. The engineer needed me!

After Cannon died, Mother gave Claiborne his toolbox. "You can tell a lot about a person from his toolbox," Claiborne said approvingly. Cannon would have liked that remark. You can tell a lot by Claiborne's toolbox too.

Though he was from Greenwood, only thirty miles from Indianola, Claiborne and I met in New Orleans. It was the fall of my junior year at Newcomb and his senior year in Civil Engineering at Mississippi State. He'd come down to New Orleans with his roommate Joe, who was dating my roommate Martha. One afternoon we were getting in the backseat of Joe's car when Claiborne noticed the scar just below my knee, the result of my 1959 car accident. "What's this?" he said, touching my scar lightly. His tone showed only curiosity. *Wow*, I thought. *He likes me, scars and all.*

The first time Claiborne took me to see his family in Greenwood, I was astounded, *enthralled* by all their activity. The Garrards are a sedate family. *Sedentary*. We sit a lot, talking or reading. But the Barnwells are standers, *movers*.

When I entered their house for the first time, Claiborne's nephew Robert, about twelve or thirteen at the time, was riding a unicycle around in a circle clockwise in the living room while Bob, Claiborne's daddy, was smoking and pacing in a circle the other way, dodging Robert and flicking his ashes in the fireplace as he passed it. Claiborne's sister Craig, an instructor in English at Southern Miss (the University of Southern Mississippi), was arranging TV trays for her sons' supper in the kitchen and bringing them to the living room—unperturbed by the pacer or the unicyclist. Claiborne's mother Gusta was cooking supper in the kitchen and bringing plates to the dining room. (She was a superb cook, better say some than her brother, Craig Claiborne, who was a prominent cookbook author and food critic for the *New York Times*.)

Only Claiborne's brother Bobby was sitting still. I sought him out when I needed a respite from motion. I met Bobby before I met Claiborne while he was in graduate school at Tulane and I was at Newcomb. He was a fixture in the student union where he *sat*, drinking coffee and socializing.

I was drawn to Claiborne even before I knew that his mother was alcoholic. But my unconscious must have known. The old alcoholic radar. In struggling with our parents' addictions, Claiborne and I became each other's allies. Humor always helps, and it is one of his best traits. He is sometimes zany-funny, sometimes silly-funny, sometimes witty-funny, and sometimes, wise-funny (my favorite).

Our relationship is complicated by having to be so many things for each other, mother, father, lover, spouse, helpmate, and friend. Communication can be difficult because we are so different. I am a word person; he is a numbers person. At times, our marriage feels like a cauldron, one hot mess of anger, blame, fear, stress, and madness. Marriage brings out all our gods, demons, habits, and blind spots. Yet love somehow overcomes.

I have failed more than I have succeeded in controlling my anger. Maybe it is understandable with Ganny at one end of the emotional spectrum, suppressing hers, and Mother at the other with her explosive rages, making it difficult to find the middle. The Buddhist writer Steven Levine says that rather than suppress our anger or react to it, we need to be aware of it, investigate it, and accept it. Another Buddhist writer, Thupten Jinpa, says we can learn to "regulate" it.

Easier said than done, but I try. Meditation helps.

◆ ◆ ◆

In the spring of 1966, Claiborne went to work for the Boeing Company on the Saturn V space rocket. I graduated from Newcomb in

May and rented an apartment with a friend across from Claiborne's on Royal Street. In the late Sixties, the Quarter was the place to be with its mix of nonconformists, peaceniks, hippies, and people of every ethnicity.

I got a summer job with the French Quarter newspaper, the *Vieux Carré Courier*, writing reviews of art gallery shows. It didn't pay much, but interviewing the artists and writing up their shows gave me the same thrill I'd felt back in sixth grade when I wrote for "Teen Tatler." In the fall I went to work teaching five-year-old children at Ferncrest, a private school with a headmistress who reminded me of the formidable headmistress of Cathedral, Miss Lee.

At the end of the summer, Caron, my Stephens roommate, and I went to England and Scotland for two weeks. When I returned, Claiborne had missed me so much he proposed. (He says I proposed to him, but it's not true.)

Mother argued for a New Orleans wedding, pointing out that it made sense because we were both working there. But the subtext was that she didn't want the bother of planning a wedding. Later, I was glad. I wouldn't have wanted childhood friends or hometown gossips to witness the alcohol-fueled behavior of the bride's parents or the groom's.

We were married on November 29, 1968, at St. George's Episcopal Church on St. Charles Avenue. Daddy had arranged for dozens of taxis to take our guests from the wedding on St. Charles Avenue to the reception at the Royal Orleans in the Quarter. He'd given directions to the first cabbie in line, but to the others he only said, "Follow that cab." When my cousin Charlotte got in the first cab, all the others followed without waiting for passengers. The rest of the party, even Claiborne and I, had to hitch rides to the reception.

After our honeymoon in Point Clear, Alabama, I moved from my apartment into Claiborne's slave-quarter apartment across the street. It had all the charm the Quarter is known for—two crumbling brick patios nestled in lush green shrubs and camellia bushes, a goldfish pond, a Buddha statue, and a banana tree that produced bananas.

Caught up in its charm, I hadn't noticed the apartment had less than adequate space and not a single, solitary closet. But, oh well. So what if the TV had to sit on top of the refrigerator? We couldn't see the snowy images anyway. When Buzz Aldrin landed on the moon, it may have been a step forward for part of mankind, but that old Philco was so many steps back, it would have made Buzz blush.

Life in that apartment was one surprise after another. The bathroom door leading out to the patio was a conversation piece. If you accidentally bumped it, it swung gaily outward, toilet paper flying. On Sundays, our upstairs tenant, a waiter at Brennan's, sometimes brought us leftovers from the famous kitchen and we had a serendipitous picnic in high style. A couple who lived in the front apartment were the first hippies I knew. The wife, whose name I've forgotten, went to work while the husband, Kenny, stayed home to take care of their two-year-old son. A house husband was unheard of in those days.

One episode may give an idea of what life was like for us in the Quarter. We were having drinks with friends on the back patio one evening when a pajamaed leg appeared on top of the wall. Amazed, we watched the rest of him gradually materialize. He took his time arranging himself cross-legged on top of the wall and began to recite a poem. I wish I could identify it. All I remember is that it had a lot of O sounds that required him to extend his arms a lot. When he'd finished, he nimbly dropped down and invited himself to sit in an empty chair in our circle. We poured him a drink.

Two months after Claiborne and I married, we gave up on the tiny apartment and moved into a two-bedroom apartment uptown on Eleanore Street, three blocks from the St. Charles Avenue streetcar. Leaving the Quarter made us sad, but there were new restaurants to discover.

I didn't appreciate food until I met Claiborne. When I was a child, I was easy to feed because all I ever wanted was half a mayonnaise sandwich. As my cousin Steve remarked recently, none of the Garrard women are cooks. Or foodies, I might add. But Claiborne came from a long line of excellent cooks.

Going to New Orleans restaurants with him was a new world. When we were broke, our favorite restaurant was the Steak Pit on Bourbon Street, where we could get soup, a hamburger steak, and a baked potato for $2.50. When we were flush, we went to Galatoire's or Elmwood Plantation on River Road, a pink mansion surrounded by a grove of lighted trees; their specialty was Oysters Mosca, its recipe rumored to have originated by the Mafia. In between those high times and low, we explored neighborhood restaurants, unpretentious and just as good as fancy ones. Aunt Marion, Uncle Jimmy, and cousins Catherine and Tom introduced us to a favorite they affectionately called "The Dump."

But we didn't spend all our time eating. We also went to the races at the Fairgrounds. The first time we went together, I won $110 in the Daily Double, a fortune to us at the time, and we tried to spend it all in one night. We invited Bobby to go with us to Commander's Palace, where we consumed more than one Orange Julius at the bar while waiting for a table. Once we were seated, we were so hungry we ordered lavishly. After all, we were rich, and Bobby loved nothing better than being treated. At the end of the meal, the waiter brought out Cherries Jubilee, and I generously offered to help ignite the flaming dessert.

One more story from our racing days because it exemplifies the era. After a losing streak at the races, Claiborne told me that Luke's Lick was going to win on Saturday. "Oh, yeah?" I said.

"It's a sure thing," he said.

"No such thing as a sure thing," I said.

But he was so sure that he agreed, if the horse lost, to buy me that outfit I wanted—mint green fleece slacks with a matching tunic top. Saturday came. Luke's Lick lost, and I got my outfit. The next Saturday, I was wearing it when the host stopped me at the door and told me, "Sorry, but ladies aren't allowed in the clubhouse in slacks."

I thanked him, went to the ladies' room, took off the slacks, smoothed the tunic, though its length bordered on indecency, and went back. This time the host waved us on with a sweeping motion and a faint smile.

Fun times, but, as always, part of me was worried about Mother and Daddy. I can hardly bear to read the stack of letters from me to them from that time. In each one, I see a daughter trying her best to live a life to please her parents, to make them happy. In a chirpy tone I no longer recognize, I would tell them about the fun we were having and didn't notice at the time that to make them happy I was reporting all the things *they* used to do. Here's one I wrote after Claiborne and I had just celebrated our one-year anniversary:

> Dear Mother and Daddy,
>
> Our visit home was so nice. We'll have to do it again sometimes. Also—our anniversary was great. We went to the races and won $55 on the second race (Claiborne's pick). Then we won $15 more (Claiborne's pick) and then the man counted out $30 instead of $15 by mistake. We didn't tell him since we figured he was giving it to us for our anniversary. Also Claiborne won $50 from his football bet at work. So we went to the Top of the Mart. As we came out, we saw a policeman getting ready to write a ticket—we were parked in a "no parking." We ran—not really hoping to stop him. But since it was our anniversary, we couldn't be anything but lucky—so he

tore up the ticket. Then we went to the Pontchartrain. Then home for a steak and our big beautiful bottle of champagne. I'd call that a nice anniversary—wouldn't you?

Claiborne was in the bottom third of the draft lottery, the group that probably won't be called. And this will definitely be his last year of Vulnerability—we must be living right!

Come to N.O. as soon as you can! Miss y'all.

Love, Marion

Races and champagne. Nothing about my struggles teaching in that first difficult year. Nothing about our worries that Claiborne's job at Boeing might be phased out.

But in 1970, that's what happened. Claiborne's project on the Saturn V at Boeing came to an end. By that time, I had quit teaching at Ferncrest (unhealthy atmosphere, domineering principal). Since my sister, Claiborne's sister, and her husband Ray all had college-teaching careers, we decided to go to graduate school at Mississippi State. Mary was always a role model, but Claiborne's sister Craig was also a big influence, showing me that it was possible to teach and raise a family. She seemed to do it with such ease and without a PhD. The graduate schools at State accepted us, Claiborne in math and me in English, and we were awarded teaching assistantships to pay our way.

Making her wishes abundantly clear for me to have children, Mother was dubious about my academic pursuits, and her doubts came out sideways. After we moved to Starkville, she gave us a chandelier and membership to the Starkville Country Club. Knee deep in studying and preparing for our classes, we barely had time to brush our teeth, much less go swim or play golf at the country club. And the chandelier? If we'd hung it from the sagging ceiling of the apartment we'd rented, we would literally have brought the house down.

In the early seventies, Daddy began having TIA (transient ischemic attacks) incidents or mini strokes, a temporary disruption in the blood supply to the brain. Possible causes were identified as high blood pressure, obesity, high cholesterol, atrial fibrillation, diabetes, and "regularly drinking an excessive amount of alcohol." Only the last one applied. Soon after we enrolled at State, these mini strokes were becoming more frequent and more debilitating. Although Daddy thought he was still managing the place, he wasn't.

In late spring when I came home for a weekend, Mother suggested that we move home to help Daddy run the farm and hinted that it was time for us to start a family. Claiborne had already begun to see that higher math wasn't what he expected. Against our better judgment, we agreed to Mother's suggestion. We finished the academic year. I finished my coursework and planned to write my thesis at home.

Our return to the Delta was the biggest mistake we ever made. At least, that's what I thought for a long time. Now, looking back, I'm not so sure.

As soon as we'd made the decision, I went into a deep depression. Every day after I'd taught classes and taken classes, I came home and went straight to bed. Unable to read or sleep, I would stare at a crack in the ceiling that forked in two directions. I could already see that I'd taken the wrong fork. It also stood for the split in me, part of me trying to make my parents happy, part looking for who I was apart from them.

Hearing of my plans, Dr. H., my Faulkner seminar professor, reminded me that "you can't go home again." I knew too much about his personal life to respect him, but his words seemed prophetic and taunted me.

One compelling reason for going back was because it looked safe. Our farming operation was lucrative, at least in those days. We would have enough money to live comfortably and raise a family. I didn't know then that nothing is safe, or not predictably safe.

When Ganny died, a woman came by our house to offer her condolences. I don't remember who she was, but like the words of my professor, hers became seared in my brain. She said she knew I'd be a loyal daughter to Mother just as Mother had been to Ganny. Yes, if loyalty meant sticking with somebody at the expense of oneself, that would be me. I had handed over an essential part of my vitality to my mother.

Chapter 27

Late for Supper

When Daddy heard we were coming home, he rose to the occasion. He moved one of his managers out of his house on a place called Les Oaks and told Joseph, his best worker, to get it ready for us. But when we got home, the house still wasn't ready, so we temporarily moved in with Mother and Daddy.

Late one afternoon, Claiborne and I drove out to see how Joseph was coming along. We noted happily that he'd already given the fence surrounding the house a coat of fresh paint. We found Joseph inside painting the living room, so we stayed to talk. Never one to watch another work, Claiborne picked up a paint brush, and I soon followed suit. Something about our painting together changed the atmosphere, and Joseph began to open up. He told us what it was like for him, as a Black man, to try to make a living and provide for his family in the Mississippi Delta. Although he was careful not to speak of his present circumstances or boss, we'd seen for ourselves how hard the laborers worked and how little they were paid. I wondered why he shared this with us, why he didn't see us as his oppressors. Maybe he felt our empathy or hoped we could do something to make things better. For whatever reason, he kept talking, we kept listening, and we all kept painting.

When we got home, Daddy had gone to bed, and Mother had fixed our supper, which at most would have been her old standby, tuna fish sandwiches, or something she'd warmed over. Though she hadn't said we needed to be home at a certain time, she must've had one in mind.

"Where were you?" she bellowed when we walked in.

"Talking to Joseph," I said.

"Talking to JOSEPH!" she yelled contemptuously.

I'd endured her explosions many times, but this time was different. "Come on. Let's go," Claiborne said, grabbing my arm. We ducked out the back door, got our things out of storage, and drove to our new home, ready or not.

By that time, I had learned a little about alcoholism. I knew that it was a disease like diabetes, and being a disease like diabetes, the alcoholic couldn't help it. But if alcoholism was a disease, and my mother had the disease, I wasn't *supposed* to hold her actions against her. I was *supposed* to try to understand her. But then, if that was true, what was I *supposed* to do with my hurt, pain, and trauma?

• • •

Any belief Claiborne and I had about the glamorous life of Delta planters was quickly dispelled. We struggled to find our niche among our peers. I worked at the town library and volunteered as a reading tutor in the predominantly Black junior high. For unexplainable reasons, an article was written for the local paper, the *Enterprise-Tocsin,* about the school, and an accompanying photo was taken of me tutoring two children. That picture didn't sit well with some. When I saw the deplorable conditions at the predominantly Black school, I began to speak out. That didn't endear me to some either, but it bonded me with a handful of others.

Because Daddy's mini strokes had affected his thinking, he left Claiborne's position undefined. He'd vaguely told Claiborne to take care of the cattle, but that was about it. As farm profits decreased, Claiborne took over the job of accountant. Uncomfortable with having assigned himself the role, he paid himself only enough for us to get by.

But we liked living in the country. Our house was three miles outside the city limits and situated on the Sunflower River. Though our well water was rust-colored, and we often got stuck on the muddy road to our house after a rain, we made the most of things.

We bought a waterbed for a sofa and a Great Dane, Tiffany, and in my memory, they will always be related. Tiffany learned to race from the kitchen through the dining room to the living room and land on the sofa/waterbed, smiling and riding the waves.

Behind the house stood an old red barn that looked just like an old red barn ought to look and inspired a watercolor painted by a friend. We planted a garden of corn, tomatoes, and green beans. We kept two horses in the pasture and set up a ping pong table in the shed. Best of all, we were within spitting distance of the Sunflower River, where the hours melted as we sat on its banks and watched the business of hawks, turtles, and waterfowl and the changing light sparkling on the water.

But if we thought we were safe in our own little corner by the river, events said otherwise. A couple of years after our return, Joseph was killed in an accident on the place. He'd been making repairs to the gin roof when he fell from a thirty-foot ladder. A tragedy for us all but catastrophic for his widow and children.

Chapter 28

Motherhood

In spite of her alcoholism and difficulty handling the day-to-day, Mother had an uncanny ability to be right about important things. She thought it was time for me to have children, and it was.

I wanted children badly, and more than anything, I wanted to be the mother my own mother wasn't and do all the things for them she didn't do for me. Being a "good mother" would take away the pain I'd suffered. Twisted, I know, but that was my thinking.

When I was pregnant with Craig, and later Will, several people told me I had an inner glow. I felt it. And when they were born, I felt happiness like no other. They were (and are) the most beautiful children in the world and precious to me. But raising them in the environment I'd chosen was a tremendous strain, and many times I couldn't or didn't give them the attention they needed. In a place where appearances and manners matter so much, raising a child to be well-behaved is no small task.

I was trying hard to do all that being a mother required and at the same time help my parents. Daddy was declining before our eyes. His mini strokes were becoming more frequent, and every time he had one, I'd drop everything and rush to his side at his house or the hospital. His face had a slack expression, and the spark had gone out of his eyes. Instead of worrying about her own poor health, her thyroid, liver issues, or her own drinking habits,

Mother projected them onto Daddy. "Sit down," she'd say to me. "Let's have a drink and talk about your daddy's drinking problem."

If I'd known how to detach from my emotions, I would have. Little by little, I was sucked into the swamp Mother and Daddy were drowning in.

Despite Mother's desire for grandchildren, once she got them, she wasn't interested. That first week out of the hospital after Craig was born, we stayed with Mother and Daddy. Her sole contribution was going to the grocery store. Eating well was important, and I was grateful. But I was disappointed that Mother didn't take the opportunity to bond with her granddaughter. Though Daddy seemed to enjoy watching my children, at least from afar, and enjoyed them more when they were old enough to play, I can't say that Mother took much pleasure in them. She too was declining. The day of Will's birth, August 9, 1976, wonderful as it was, woke me up to their decline. After they'd visited us in the Greenville hospital, a nurse who'd seen them standing at the nursery window asked me if they were my grandparents. They were in their early sixties.

• • •

Soon after Craig was born, I found a babysitter who had the inner calm of St. Francis. Hattie Harrington was a middle-aged African American woman whose father worked for Daddy. Her calm was contagious, and I am grateful for every atom that rubbed off on me. She would later be a babysitter for Will too and then a sitter for Daddy after the kids went to school. She was a wise woman. If I was going out with friends but reluctant to leave my children, she reassured me by saying, "You go on. You'll have fun once you get there."

I'll never forget the time I went inside Hattie's house for something. She was sitting in front of the TV with a baby in her lap and

Our children: William Garrard Barnwell and Augusta Craig Barnwell at four and seven

a child nestled in each arm. One of the children had put a hat on Hattie's head that would've looked silly on someone else but on her it looked regal. Those grandbabies of hers had an aura of contentment that can't be manufactured. Hattie's calm vibes would have tamed a tiger. After she died, I was told by one of her daughters that Hattie's lifelong wish had been to go to Disneyworld. In her eighties, she got that wish and died while on one of the rides. It wouldn't surprise me if she planned it that way.

Despite the outings Hattie made possible, much of the time in Craig's first months, I was lonely. We lived only a few miles from town, but those few miles meant no drop-in company. Claiborne worked when his employees worked and often didn't come home until well after dark. It was time to move.

A few months before Will was born, we bought a house. It was on Percy Street, named for Walker Percy's kin. I took it to be a good sign. Now Craig would have playmates and sidewalks for her Big Wheel, and I would have community. It was three blocks from my parents' house, and in a pinch, I could leave the kids with Annie.

Mother's contribution in helping was picking Craig up and taking her to the grocery store. Though I was grateful for time alone with Will, the outing was always near noon. At the store, she'd buy Craig any candy bar she wanted and let her eat it on the spot. Then back they came in time for Craig not to eat her lunch.

• • •

Once we moved to Percy Street, I became close to the neighborhood mothers. Every day after naptime, we took the children to a nearby park. From their three-foot vantage point, the kids couldn't see anything but the jeans we all wore, so it was not unusual for someone else's kid to hug my knees. I loved that. If I was a "good enough Mother," I owe a lot to the other mothers—my friends and role models. My heroes.

• • •

Though his work made it impossible for Claiborne to help with the day-to-day rearing of our children, he made up for it through his sense of play and inventiveness. Once when school was unexpectedly cancelled, I picked up Will, Craig, and a friend of Craig's and took them home. It was raining and the kids were grumpy because the rain had ruined their plans. Then Claiborne showed up, the rain having sidelined him too. Instead of listening to their complaints, he decided he'd make hot tamales and we would help him. He lined us up assembly-line fashion at the kitchen counter—Craig, her playmate, Will, and me—and gave us each a part in the production. I don't remember if the hot tamales were any good, but that was beside the point.

The Sunflower River was again a reprieve from the usual routine. With the help of our friend Lanny, Claiborne built an A-frame in

Claiborne and Will in father-son golf tournament in Cambrian Ridge, Alabama, in 2011

a stand of woods along the bank, a perfect spot to set up camp, cook s'mores, and tell stories. He also built a pontoon boat for exploring the river. On the first trip out, we made our friends take off their muddy shoes before stepping onto our swabbed deck, and we lined them up on the foredeck. But when we motored away, the front of the boat dipped, and it was goodbye to twelve pairs of good tennis shoes.

But as helpful as these times were when Claiborne stepped in, I was the one who read the kids stories, made lemonade for their lemonade stand, swept their playhouse, taught them to ride a bike, and took them to all their activities. We spent many summer afternoons at our dear friend Eleanor's pool. I took Will fishing when Claiborne wasn't available. Will was so happy to be going, he forgave me for using pop-tops for bait and didn't seem to mind when we didn't catch anything. When Craig first learned to drive, she asked me to hide in the backseat of the car so she could pretend to her friends she was driving unsupervised. I did.

Most of their teenage years were a matter of survival. On a day in late summer when they needed new clothes for school, I took them to the mall in Jackson to shop. Craig had her license by then and was begging to drive. Sensing that I needed to keep what power I could, I sat firmly in the driver's seat. After a long day of shopping, we got back in the car and started on the two-hour drive home. They had reached the silly stage, the loud, obnoxious, sing-loud-as-we-can-and turn-up-the-radio-as-high-as-it-will-go-so-we-can't-hear-Mama-fussing stage. By the time we got to Yazoo City, I was ready to check into the nearest sanitorium. Then there was a Divine intervention. We were stopped at a railroad crossing waiting for a train to pass when I took a hard look at the car in front of us and saw it was Ellen, our neighbor and my friend. Oh, yes, by God, it was.

I shifted into "park" and opened my door. The kids stopped singing to stare at me. "You drive, Craig," I said, getting out. "I'll see y'all at home." I got in the car with Ellen.

• • •

Ray, our brother-in-law, was the one who prompted us to tell our kids about alcoholism that plagued both sides of their family. We had gone to visit him and Claiborne's sister Craig in Ocean Springs. The kids were downstairs when Ray said, "You have told them, haven't you?" He pointed downstairs.

No. We hadn't. Having both been raised in denials and twisted thinking, we hadn't told them. It took Ray, whose family had been spared the disease, to see our lapse. After he'd set us straight, we told our children their family histories of alcoholism. Thank goodness for Ray.

Chapter 29

Endings, Beginnings

In 1978, Mother and I went to Greenwood to my Aunt Mary Jayne's annual Literary Seminar to hear the esteemed writer Willie Morris. I don't know what made Mother decide to go with me; by then, she rarely went anywhere except the grocery store, the beauty shop, or to take Daddy riding to see the crops.

Willie's mother had died the year before: the previous April, to be exact. "The death of the last of one's parents is one of life's great divides," he said. He spoke about the difficulties inherent in any parent-child relationship. As only Willie could do, he moved us all to tears.

Mother died on April 6, within days of the seminar. She'd gone to the hospital with chest pains and was diagnosed with congestive heart failure. Since the disease is usually not life-threatening, the doctor had put her in a regular room instead of the ICU.

On one of my daily visits, Mother worried aloud about the Mahonia bushes that grew near the patio. "I didn't prune them," she said, regret heavy in her voice. It was an odd thing for her to say since she'd never pruned them herself, and yet she'd distinctly said "I." Later, I saw that she might have meant she regretted not having pruned them herself, and if that was so it was an admission that she regretted not being more engaged in her own life.

On a magnificent spring day, Craig and I were sitting outside on the patio in sun lounges, hers a miniature of mine, pretending we were at the beach. She was six. Will, age two at the time, was sleeping in his crib near a door I'd left open so I could hear him if he woke up.

When a shadow appeared in the passageway between the patio and garage, I couldn't make out who it was. The figure stepped into the light, and I saw that it was Mother's doctor. He motioned me over. He told me that Mother had died. I shook my head. *No, that's not true. It couldn't be. Because it's a perfect spring day.*

When Mother talked about the Mahonia bushes, I think she foresaw her death. She foresaw it, but her doctor and I had both missed it.

A few weeks after her death, I wrote a letter to Willie in Bridgehampton, New York, and told him of her death. I told him that, in retrospect, his words about his mother had been prescient. I told him that all the things he couldn't say to his mother were the same things I couldn't say to mine but that I felt I *had* said them—through him.

He wrote me back. The letter he sent me had no street address, just Indianola, Mississippi, but I got it. He said, "I know what you mean. There are things unsaid between a parent and a child which are really the most important things of all, I believe."

• • •

In *Shadow Dance*, David Richo says:

> Our problem is not that our needs were unmet by our parents but that they are unmourned by us now in the present. Once we do the personal work of mourning the shadow side of our past, its deficiencies, or abuses, we have greater access to the enriching intimacy others may provide.[1]

It took me a long time to learn how to grieve. When Mother died, I made a start, or rather Mary and I made a start together. We only thought we'd been close before. We talked, we cried, we laughed, told stories, laughed some more, cried some more. Losing Daddy three years later was just as traumatic, but by then we knew what to do—talk, cry, laugh, tell stories.

• • •

When I was young, I couldn't allow myself to see my mother's good side. To see her beneath the disease was like watching the moon landing through snow.

Now, finally, I can see her good qualities. I also see some of her worst qualities in myself, tough to bear. Thinking deeply about Mother's life and seeing what she left incomplete has been difficult and painful, but it has given me direction.

• • •

Since I was a front-row witness to my mother's problematic life, you'd think I'd have avoided, at all costs, her life choices. But instead, I put myself into the very same situation: Here I was married to a man who farmed the same land as Daddy; I had two children, and no creative outlets. What was I thinking? I had put myself in the very circumstances that suffocated her, and I would either die—or find my way. A risky business.

But that's how I did it. Scared myself to pieces and found my way. I got a job.

It saved my life.

Chapter 30

Love, Work, and Friends

In 1979, the year after mother died, I began teaching at Delta State University in Cleveland, Mississippi, thirty miles from Indianola. I was hired as a tutor in the Writing Center and as an instructor for two sections of Junior English, a remedial composition class for students with weak writing skills. It was challenging to teach the remedial class, grade papers, and work one-on-one with students in the Writing Center. The position was considered part-time, and I was paid less because of it. I didn't care. I loved what I was doing. "They're paying me to read!" I told my family.

I was able to coordinate my schedule with the kids'. Will attended three-year-old preschool two days a week and stayed with Daddy and Hattie on the other three days. Craig was in first grade, and I was able to get home in time to pick her up.

Delta State University is a hidden gem. Some of the students were first-generation college students, while older ones came back for a degree to advance their careers. Both set a high bar in the classroom. At DSU, football is not an obsession. A few years ago, a fan of DSU football facetiously named the mascot "The Fighting Okra" in the spirit of "let's not take this football business too seriously," and it stuck.

In the spring of 1981, after I'd been teaching part-time for two years, a full-time tenured position opened. I wanted it, but I knew it would be sought after and that I'd have to be competitive. To prove myself, I asked Dr. S., the chair of the department, if I could teach a summer term of sophomore literature, a course difficult to fill—too many papers to grade and too much material to cover in too little time. Luckily, I drew a particularly lively class of engaged students, so I screwed up my courage and asked Dr. S. to observe the class, hoping it would sway him to give me the full-time position.

In the days before Dr. S.'s visit, I lay on my sofa, and channeled Mrs. Davis, my teacher from Cathedral. I used creative visualization, picturing myself and my students in a lively discussion. The day's assignment would be Browning's "My Last Duchess," a dramatic monolog that appealed to students. I tipped off the class beforehand and asked them to continue doing their best.

Things were going well. Being privy to what was going on and invested in the outcome, the kids were engaged. I'd never seen so many hands go up. But after observing the class for a third of the ninety-minute session, Dr. S. got up, nodded briefly, and left.

After class, I went by his office to find out what had gone wrong. He told me I was a good teacher, better than he was, and said I had the job. That fall I was assigned two sections of Freshman Composition and two sections of Sophomore Literature, and as a full-time employee, I would be paid accordingly.

◆ ◆ ◆

Freud believed that love and work were the main things, but somewhere along the line, someone added "friendship." Whoever it was was right. At Delta State, I found my tribe. Though technically, we were the Department of English in the *Division* of Languages and Literature, we were not divided. We were a feisty group with differing points of view, but most of the time, we were willing to collaborate. Unlike many departments I've heard about, we didn't backbite. My colleagues and I shared a student-centered philosophy that encouraged more interaction, less correction, and more emphasis on the positive.

In the mid-1980s, a member of the board of trustees challenged our decision to teach Alice Walker's 1982 novel *The Color Purple*, objecting ostensibly to explicit sexual content. The dean called a meeting. Knowing the objection was probably the theme of racial injustice that had offended the board member, my colleagues and I gathered for a meeting before the meeting to strategize. When the dean walked into the conference room, he stopped to stare when he saw us. All of us were wearing purple—purple sweaters, purple ties, purple slacks, purple jackets, purple socks, purple shirts, purple scarves. "I didn't get the memo," he protested with a grin. "Meeting adjourned."

One of the stories I loved to teach was James Baldwin's "Sonny's Blues." In the climactic scene, the protagonist goes to a nightclub to hear his estranged brother, Sonny, play the piano and sing. When Sonny sings "Am I Blue?" all the trouble between them drops away. It's a powerful story. Every semester I'd ask my students if they knew the song "Am I Blue?" None ever did. And none had a recording either until the semester I had Eden Brent in my class, a talented blues singer and musician at the beginning of her career. She said, "I can get one. My mother used to sing in a New York nightclub. I could ask her to sing it, and I'll play the piano and record it. Okay?" More than okay, Eden. From then on, along with the story, I played my recording of Carole Brent singing "Am I Blue" with Eden's accompaniment on the piano.

We were a good department, but when Dorothy Shawhan became chair, we were better. A writer herself, she encouraged us never to let our jobs get in the way of our creative pursuits. Spirits high, we returned to our artistic projects. We invited noted writers to come visit our campus and read from their work, and they came. Among them were Adrienne Rich, Ernest J. Gaines,

James Whitehead, Willie Morris, Richard Ford, Margaret Walker Alexander, Elizabeth Spencer, Larry Brown, Lewis Nordan, Richard Lederer, Brooks Haxton, and Ellen Douglas.

In 1988, Dorothy and I founded *Tapestry*, an annual faculty literary magazine that we called in our preface "a faculty celebration of words." Along with editing, Dorothy and I contributed a piece of writing in each issue—and so did most of the faculty. Supportive members from the Art Department created professionally designed covers, each one a work of art.

Tapestry wove us together as faculty and deepened our ties to the Delta community. My Aunt Mary Jayne was a gracious supporter and often came from Greenwood to help celebrate a new issue. We held our annual celebration at various homes in the Delta. Emma Lytle's home was one, a rambling, comfortable farmhouse at Perthshire Plantation in Gunnison, a few miles north of Cleveland. Known for her paintings of local scenes, particularly African American baptisms, Emma was also a poet and would sometimes read us her poems at these gatherings. Keith Somerville Dockery McLean also hosted our *Tapestry* parties at her home on iconic Dockery Plantation on the Sunflower River, the place where legendary blues musicians once sang and played, among them Charley Patton, "Honeyboy" Edwards, and "Howlin' Wolf" Burnett.

Most of the time, these occasions were harmonious, a time to appreciate each other's works. But on one occasion at Dockery, our department poet read a few too many poems in appreciation of doves to suit the art professor, who was a hunter. When the department poet had finished reading his poems, the artist-hunter stood up and in a loud voice began to read passages from his hunting journal. Doves were mentioned. After he read a particularly graphic passage in which he shot them, the air filled up with heated words and then—a deadly silence. And some pointed glares. Out of nowhere a laugh bubbled up that came from Keith's husband

Hite. It was a conciliatory laugh. A contagious laugh. The shoulders of the department poet began to shake in suppressed laughter. The artist-hunter smiled. The department poet chuckled. The artist-hunter laughed. The party continued.

◆ ◆ ◆

When they hear Edward Elgar's "Pomp and Circumstance," most people think about their own graduation. But when I hear it, I think about how we faculty were required to march with the graduates every year. Pressed to get our grades turned in on time, everyone fussed about it, including me. But now when I hear it, I think about the deep kinship I felt toward my colleagues at Delta State and about a career I was lucky to find.

Chapter 31

1981

After Mother's death, Daddy became more confused. He would often wander about the house calling for Mother. Sometimes he thought I was Mother.

He was agitated. To calm him, I took him riding around town and out on the place. He seemed to relax when the cotton fields came into view and looked alert as he gazed out the window. These glimpses of him like he'd been before the strokes made me sad, made me happy. I bought myself a pair of rose-colored sunglasses.

When he no longer could fix himself a drink, he inexplicably forgot about it. No longer obsessed with alcohol, he'd fixate on other things. Out of the blue he'd insist on going to see a friend who was no longer with us. Or he'd say he was supposed to meet somebody to play golf or poker. One day, he said he had to see somebody in Monteagle, Tennessee, where our family had vacationed four decades earlier. I knew this somebody was no longer there.

I didn't know what to do. The doctors had advised me to try to keep Daddy in reality by telling him regularly the day, date, and time and by reminding him of where he was and what was going on. But on this day, no matter what cues I gave him, he insisted he had to go to Monteagle. About this time, Daddy's nephew Garrard walked in unexpectedly. He's the one who'd receive a special meal at Rosemary, the hamburger I'd coveted. Some say he was the black sheep of the family, but it wasn't true. He had a good heart and a sixth sense about when his presence was needed. We hadn't seen him in a year or two, but he greeted us as if we'd seen him yesterday. He squeezed my arm and crossed the room to shake Daddy's hand. "Hey, Uncle Billy," he said. "What's happening?"

"I need to go to Monteagle," Daddy told him.

"Well, let's go," said Garrard. "Okay if we go in my car?"

Daddy didn't wait for me to help him from his wheelchair into the car. After saying goodbye, I went back inside and told Hattie that Daddy had gone on a road trip to Tennessee. She nodded knowingly.

Thirty minutes later, Garrard opened the kitchen door and maneuvered Daddy's wheelchair inside.

"How was your trip?" I asked Daddy.

"Fine. Fine," he said, all business.

Sometimes reality is overrated.

• • •

On October 24, 1981, Daddy slipped into a coma and was admitted to the hospital. That night, a Saturday, I went to the hospital alone. Before going to Daddy's room, I bought myself a Coke from the vending machine down the hall. I rarely drank them and wondered why I'd bought it. On the first sip, I remembered. I saw us again, me a child with one hand on Daddy's shoulder, the other holding a Coke.

When I entered Daddy's room, his nurse shook her head, meaning he was still in a coma. She got up, gathered her things, and left me alone with him. I climbed up on the hospital bed and sat beside him. I realized that for the first time in a long time, I felt free of worry. I leaned in and said, "Go on if you need to. I'll be all right." I knew they were the words I had to say because, otherwise, the politest boy in school would have stayed.

He died the next day, October 25, 1981. I was grateful to be there with him, having missed being with Mother when she died. Claiborne and Dr. Lanny were also there, and we surrounded his bed, making a circle to ease him out of this life and into the next. We held his funeral at his home on Barberry Lane. Barely five years old at the time, Will sat by me until midway through the service and then moved to sit by Mary. An act of diplomacy that reminded me of Daddy.

My father was a man of contradictions. He was an unreconstructed southerner who was nevertheless loved and respected by his Black employees. For a man who lost unfairly a sister and two brothers, a man who lived in the shadow of a highly successful man, a man with an untreated addiction and a wife who also suffered from addiction *and* depression, Daddy did the best he could.

We were partners, two fingers, just like that.

Chapter 32

End of an Era

In 1985, we quit farming. It was a slow death, having begun in 1981 when the price of cotton was low, and the cost of production high. We'd reached the breaking point several times but hung on by streamlining the operation and economizing wherever possible. When Claiborne asked our accountant, Robert, whom we both greatly respected, what he thought we should do, he said, "Well, Claiborne, the first thing you should do is quit."

So we did. We faced our debts and figured out how to pay them off. Before we rented out the land, Claiborne put the equipment up for sale. The day of the sale, he told me not to go, so I didn't. My dear cousin Charlotte came over from Greenwood to give him moral support. I'll never forget that. Every time a piece of equipment was sold for a fraction of what it was worth, Charlotte would say, "It's just stuff, Claiborne. Just stuff."

A few months after the sale, Claiborne and I found ourselves watching a TV show on the devastating history of slavery and sharecropping. He was sitting in a chair, and I was on the sofa across the room. When the program was over, we got up and crossed the room to hug each other. We held each other for a long time and cried. Tears of relief. We were out of it.

In 1981, to give the workers something to do when the crops were laid by, Claiborne had planted a vineyard of French American hybrid and vinifera grapes. In 1985 we opened a boutique winery,

Claiborne Vineyards, and the sideline venture brought accolades from wine experts and customers alike. In the same year, Claiborne went back into the field he was trained for, civil engineering, and went to work for the Mississippi Department of Transportation (MDOT) in Indianola.

We moved into the house on Barberry Lane. What had once been unthinkable now seemed the thing to do. I wanted our children to grow up enjoying the bayou with its bronze and stately cypress trees. I wanted them to watch the turtles traverse our yard to bury their eggs. I wanted them to enjoy, as I had, croquet matches on the lawn.

Before we moved in, we remodeled the kitchen and tried to make it more functional. We made the house our own however we could, but the truth was it would always be my parents' home. After living there sixteen years, we sold it after Claiborne took a job with the Environmental Division of MDOT in Jackson, Mississippi.

For the next five years, except for a sabbatical, I continued to teach at Delta State. I rented an apartment and arranged a four-day schedule so that Claiborne and I would have long weekends together. I retired in May of 2003. In June, our daughter presented us with our first grandchild, Joshua. Jane Claiborne was born two years later. They live only twenty minutes from our home in Jackson and I am grateful to be involved in their daily lives. They are blessings beyond compare. They call me "Gan."

Chapter 33

The Delta, Part Three

We were having drinks at Chris's. Chris and her sister Jessie had asked us to come, three couples, Claiborne and I, Cynthia and Jimmy, and Barbara and Lanny. It was a lovely summer evening in Chris's beautiful garden of roses and day lilies. The birds were chattering in the crepe myrtles that bordered the garden.

At nightfall, someone in the group brought up the subject of our racially divided town and what to do about it. The conversation was familiar but then took a turn when one of us said, "What's the date of B.B.'s concert this year?" (B.B. King was called B.B. to his friends and B. to his close friends.) Jimmy consulted his calendar.

"What if . . . ?" Chris began. "What if we have a party?" We waited, sensing more to come. "What if we have a party for B.B.?"

We were stunned into silence.

"Well, if we do it," Jimmy said, "we'll need to include guests from the Black community."

"My thoughts exactly," said Chris. "Why not have it right here? In this garden?"

Slowly we began to see how it might work. If anybody could get away with a biracial party, it would be Chris. Having served for years as president of the local bank, she was a highly respected member of the Black and White communities. The rest of us offered to cohost. Maybe we'd pass muster: Jessie ran a successful shoe store; Lanny was a doctor; Barbara was a nurse; Jimmy was the editor of the town newspaper; Cynthia was its managing editor; Claiborne, a farmer; and I, a teacher.

We enlisted our Black friends and White friends to help us come up with a racially balanced guest list. When we'd completed it, we had 125 people to invite, including a man who had once been a member of the White Citizens' Council and a man who was the assistant principal at the Black Junior High.

We had the usual preparty jitters. Should we serve wine or liquor or both? Who should we ask to cater? Was the list really okay? Had we left anyone out? *Would they come?*

They did.

During the party, I kept watching B B., hoping he was having a good time. I needn't have worried. Every time I checked, he was in the middle of a different group, all smiling, or laughing with abandon. Birds chirped in trees, lanterns lit up the garden, the champagne flowed, and our spirits soared.

Though Jimmy insisted we keep the media out during the party, the next morning blues historian Robert Palmer interviewed several hosts and attendees for a piece that would appear the next morning, June 11, 1983, on the front page of the *New York Times*. Those he quoted remarked that everyone mingled and had a good time. In his interview, B.B. said, "I do know that although I've been back to Indianola a number of times, last night, being able to shake hands with the elite of Indianola on a social basis, well, that was my real homecoming."[1]

The next morning, Diane Sawyer introduced "CBS Sunday Morning" with Ed Rabel doing an interview with B.B. Rabel noted that a two-lane street had just been renamed "B.B. King Street" and asked B.B. how it made him feel. B.B. said the road gave him a good feeling, "[b]ut the remarkable part of the celebration happened here in this private garden in Indianola, where some of the town's most prominent citizens threw a party for B.B. King."[2]

I didn't kid myself that one party would change anything, but it was not nothing. It was an overture. A time for Black guests to meet White guests, and White guests to meet Black guests. An opportunity for people to meet B.B. Shake his hand. See his smile. Hear his laugh. Human exchanges that can leave an impression, change a mind.

• • •

B.B. King was born in the tiny community of Berclair, Mississippi, but considered Indianola his hometown. He gave free concerts in B.B. King park for the four years prior to his death in 2015.

On September 13, 2008, the B.B. King Museum and Delta Interpretive Center opened. It is a highly esteemed, state-of-the-art museum that draws huge crowds from all over the world. In the same year that it opened, B.B. bought Club Ebony and donated it to the museum. It was the place where, after his free concerts in the park, B.B. wrapped up the event by playing to a standing-room-only audience. It is a landmark where famous blues artists from the forties, fifties, and sixties stopped to perform while on "the chitlin' circuit," that included not only B.B. but also Ray Charles, Count Basie, Bobby Bland, Little Milton, Albert King, James Brown, Ike Turner, Howlin' Wolf, and many others.

Chapter 34

Dorothy

When Dorothy Shawhan died in 2014, the world seemed awfully empty. She'd been my friend, my colleague, my boss, my fellow writer, and so much more.

While on a trip to Machu Picchu in 2014, the altitude was too much for her lungs. Born with scoliosis, she had breathing issues and contracted pneumonia shortly after her return. Her doctor put a breathing tube in her nose and tethered her to an oxygen machine. She didn't like it. She would go through the house dragging the machine and cry, "More cord! More cord!" It was a playful reference to an experiment conjured up by a colleague in the physics department, and although I never understood its workings, it involved something called a "hover craft" and prompted the students to cry, "More cord. More Cord."

Just like Ganny two generations before, Dorothy grew up in Verona and Tupelo, Mississippi. Discovering our common heritage was only one of our many bonds.

Dorothy taught writing and literature classes at Delta State for twenty-five years, and for fourteen of those years she was chair of the Division of Languages and Literature. Among her many awards, she was recognized by the American Association of University Women (AAUW), Mississippi University for Women Alumna of the Year, DSU's Kossman Outstanding Teacher of the Year, and Mississippi Humanities Council Educator of the Year.

Dorothy was a storyteller. She could both tell and write a story with the best of them. She had compassion for women whose accomplishments had been overlooked or diminished by a disinterested culture and wrote about them in many of her short stories, her three nonfiction books, an eBook, and one novel, *Lizzie*. Based on real people, *Lizzie* is about a Mississippi governor's daughter born in 1902 in Clarksdale (Mississippi). The governor raises her to have the political drive of the son he wanted, and that's where her troubles begin. Though Dorothy never thought it, she was also a woman whose tremendous accomplishments were overlooked. *Lizzie* should have won a major literary prize.

• • •

After Dorothy died, I wrote the following entry in my journal:

> What is this grief like? Sometimes it's so tender and I'm open and see the beauty and the love and the preciousness of life. And somehow that becomes the toughest part. I'm only grieving for Dorothy a little bit because she lived her life as she wanted and died as she chose—not to be tethered to a machine.
>
> So this grief of mine is mostly for me. Bereft that I won't be present to that lovely spirit at least in its earthly form.
>
> The times when I let grief in are actually the good times. The times I run away from it are the worst. . . . The most positive moments are those when I'm inspired to be more like Dorothy. So unselfish. So unconcerned about self. . . . Grief has its own pattern and I am helpless in its grip—and maybe that's the point.

• • •

About two weeks after Dorothy died, I went to see my massage therapist. I'd postponed the appointment for Dorothy's funeral and told Travis why I had to change it. When I arrived at his office, he greeted me and asked how I was. I began to tell him about my knee and hip when he stopped me, saying, "No. I mean how are *you*?" He meant how was I taking my loss. Sensing that I was shaky and queasy, he said: "Let's do something different."

He cleared the room of negative energy with sage, put on a drum recording, and asked me to lie face down on the table. Minutes later, I began to cry. I felt Dorothy nearby. She told me to let go, to let her go. I cried harder.

I began to emit wild animal sounds I didn't recognize. Then I did. They sounded like birth pangs, and they seemed to go on and on. I was grieving Dorothy's death, but I was also grieving some very old wounds. After a while, I sat up. Travis was sitting on a counter across the room. He looked at me and smiled in a way that meant, "All is well." My heart was wide open, but I felt no shame, only safety, security, and love.

• • •

Soon after the session with Travis, an image came to me. Just this: Dorothy floating. In a journal entry dated January 30, 2015, I wrote:

> There was only one way to free herself, a drastic one, but I don't think she was afraid. She was released on December 21, 2014, the Winter Solstice, the darkest day of the year. When she left us, it was darker still. But not for her. She was climbing the light-filled stars and floating high above us.

• • •

On a trip to New Orleans a few months after Dorothy died, I happened into a place called B.E.E. Gallery and became entranced with a painting by Martin LaBorde. I bought three of his prints. In each one, a figure is floating. In the first one, he floats on the back of a crocodile; in the other two, he floats up into a big sky. I couldn't take my eyes off the prints.

I didn't connect the images with Dorothy until later when I happened to reread the January 30 journal entry. At the time, I had been too spellbound by LaBorde to make the connection. When I asked the gallery manager what more he could tell me about LaBorde, he pointed to a stack of small books LaBorde wrote called *The Magic Book of Bodo*.[1] I added it to my purchases and started reading.

LaBorde was born deaf, but when he discovered that his handicap enhanced his visual sense, he became an artist. In his early twenties, after a successful surgery on his ears, with the help of hearing aids, his hearing was restored but his painting output diminished. Hoping to reignite his imagination, he took a trip to Teotihuacan, Mexico, where he became intrigued by the Pyramid of the Sun in the Valley of Mexico. At 216 feet high, and 7,500 feet above sea level, it is the tallest pyramid in the western hemisphere. Although he was not physically equipped to climb the thigh-high steps, he climbed them anyway.

At the pinnacle, he heard a strange whistling through his hearing aids and then began to hear stories, ancient stories, wise stories, stories of wonder and magic. Afterwards, he felt a deep sense of peace. He felt "transfigured" and found himself in a place where "[t]here was no I. No me." Out of this nowhere, a vision emerged of a comical figure *floating* toward him. He wore a colorful robe and a conical hat and carried a wand with a star on the tip. When LaBorde asked the figure who he was, he answered "Bodo." When LaBorde asked, "What do you want from me?" Bodo answered, "You already know."[2]

After that trip to Mexico, Bodo appeared in every sketch he made. If LaBorde tried to erase him, he'd reappear. Magic. Wonder. A phase of enormous creativity followed.

Now I saw that when Dorothy was released first from the oxygen machine and then from her body, she floated up—just like she did in my dream—into a great big LaBorde sky.

Chapter 35

Annie's Time

After Daddy died, our cook, Annie, was able to retire and continue to live in her home alone. A few years ago, when her arthritic knee made it difficult for her to walk, I went through the process of obtaining home health services for her. It was the least I could do after she'd worked for my family for thirty years.

One requirement was for her to have a physical exam and a doctor's referral. On the day of the 11 a.m. appointment, I reached Indianola early to make sure she was ready. At 10:30 she was sipping orange juice, still in her gown. At 10:45 she was sipping orange juice, still in her gown, and in no hurry. This is why she's lived so long, and I'll die before my time, I thought. At 11:00 I called the clinic and said we'd be late. At 11:15 I told Annie it was time to go. "Humpf," she said. "I haven't seen the doctor yet that had to wait on me."

Though it was almost noon before we got there, she was right. She had not kept the doctor waiting. She'd come to work at our house promptly for over thirty years, and she was now on "Annie's time."

On May 30, 2018, Annie turned *one hundred*. Claiborne, Craig, the grandchildren, and I went to her church for her birthday celebration. The church was filled to overflowing. A bright sun streamed through clear glass windows. The deacons sat reverently on the left side of the altar, and the elect group of Mothers, dressed in white, sat on the right, looking regal.

We kept looking back for Annie. Noting our apprehension, the lady next to me whispered, "She'll be here."

The choir sang a hymn. I looked around again for Annie. A tall, young man, beanpole-thin, took a seat at a piano in the corner. Reverend Turner stepped up to the pulpit. In his black-framed glasses, he looked more professor than preacher. In a low but compelling voice Reverend Turner began to speak. At the conclusion of each salient point, the piano player struck a chord. Thirty minutes into the sermon, I heard some rustling at the back of the church. Annie had arrived. Reverend Turner stopped midsentence, took off his glasses, and gestured toward her. "Here she is," he said with a look of relief and wonder.

In a white lace dress and a corsage of pink roses, she looked more like a bride than a centenarian. Walking slowly down the aisle with the help of her walker, she stopped again and again to wave, squeeze a shoulder, or grab a hand. His sermon forgotten, Reverend Turner draped an arm across the pulpit and benignly watched Annie's progress.

When Annie was settled on the front row, he picked up his sermon where he'd left off. He'd been talking about the sinful woman who washed Jesus' feet. When he shifted abruptly from the foot washing to a description of a blind woman he'd seen on a bus, I thought I'd missed something. I looked at the piano player, and he looked puzzled too. When Reverend Turner shifted the subject again, this time to an old man counting nickels for his grandson's milk at a convenience store, I worried that Annie's late entrance had rattled him. But then, Reverend Turner tied everything together by saying, "Brothers and Sisters, I'm talking about love. Love of a woman who washed the feet of the Lord. Love for a blind woman given a seat on a bus. Love for a man counting nickels." An extra loud bang on the piano. "Love that is sometimes nearly missed." Another chord on the piano. "Love that looks like this sometimes and that another. Brothers and sisters, we must be always on the lookout for love in all its man-i-fes-ta-tions." Another chord, this one held till the vibration faded.

Though they didn't look alike, Reverend Turner, in his sermon on love, reminded me of another preacher, Reverend Wheeler Parker, Emmett Till's cousin who had been with him on the fateful 1955 trip from Chicago to Money, Mississippi. I met Reverend Parker while on a bus tour of the Mississippi Delta. A warm, open, and friendly man. "Aren't you bitter?" I asked when I learned who he was. "Couldn't afford to be. It would've killed me," he said. [See Addendum E.]

Before the service was over, a stranger with wild eyes burst in through the church doors and yelled, "I don't want no handout." Walking unevenly, he headed down the aisle. I'd noticed him before the service, passing around a hat. Reverend Turner tried to put a hand on the man's shoulder, but the stranger batted it away. When Reverend Turner invited him to become a member of the church, the man nonsensically repeated, "I don't want no handout." Despite his protests, several hands reached in pockets and purses. Reverend Turner put up a restraining hand, told the congregation to keep their money, and asked if anyone had a job for "our brother." Several hands went up, but the man shook his head and strode back down the aisle and out of the church, slamming the door behind him. A hush fell over us as we thought about what had just happened. Among them was this: Reverend Turner had shown the stranger the very love he'd been preaching about.

At Annie's reception, everybody had a story to tell me about Annie, things I never knew. How she had made baptismal gowns for the babies, cooked dinner for the sick, given her time and money to the needy, and befriended the stranger. It wasn't hard to figure out where Reverend Turner had learned about love.

Though she may do it in her own time and not in any showy way, Annie is a mother to us all. At this writing, she is 105 years old. When I go by to see her, she says, "You're my little girl." Then imitating my child-voice, she hollers, "Annie! Lemme cut out the biscuits."

Chapter 36

The Unveiling

At the request of the Mississippi Arts Commission, I wrote the text for a Writers Trail Marker for my sister, Mary. The marker was unveiled on June 26, 2023, at the Henry M. Seymour Library in Indianola. It stands at the corner of Percy and Moody Streets. Here's the text:

> Mary Dubose Garrard, Professor Emerita at American University in Washington, D.C., was born in 1937 and grew up in Indianola. A preeminent art historian, Dr. Garrard received degrees from Newcomb College, Harvard University, and Johns Hopkins University. Her groundbreaking 1989 book on 17th-century Italian painter Artemisia Gentileschi launched modern studies of the now-famous artist; her third book on Artemisia (2020) positioned the artist among feminist writers of her time. In *Brunelleschi's Egg* (2010) Garrard examined the intersecting forces of nature, art, and gender in Renaissance Italy. With her partner Norma Broude, Garrard produced four volumes of feminist scholarship in art history. In 2010 American University colleagues established a feminist art history conference in honor of Broude and Garrard. On receiving a Lifetime Achievement Award from the Mississippi Institute of Arts and Letters (2011), Garrard said, "There are those who leave and those who stay. It's a big divide, but we all have Mississippi in our souls."

Mary, Craig, and I standing in front of Mary's Writers Trail marker unveiling in Indianola, June 26, 2023

The unveiling at the Seymour Library was a wonderful celebration of Mary's accomplishments. Many of our old friends were there, some from as far away as Oxford and Pontotoc, and we met some new ones. Except for Will, who'd just moved to Washington state, our immediate family were all there, along with some boyfriends, girlfriends, and more friends.

Mary Ann Griffin, executive director of the Sunflower County Libraries, officially welcomed us from the podium inside the library. City alderman Sam Brock welcomed us on behalf of the mayor and other aldermen. In a compelling African American rhythm, he quoted the last sentence of Mary's marker. After I introduced Mary, she talked about growing up in Indianola. One part of her talk stands out:

> And then I grew up and left, but Indianola was in my bones. A small town that nurtured people with big ideas—from B.B. King to Craig Claiborne, but also to one of the founders of

the infamous racist White Citizen's Council, who was our neighbor. The best and the worst lived side by side, yet we all got our mail at 38751. Indianola's street plan and its culture imprinted us equally, if differently on both sides of the tracks.

• • •

When Mary published her monumental book *Artemisia Gentileschi*, it is astounding but accurate to say that she and only a few other scholars researching women artists changed the course of art history.[1] She reclaimed for history a long-ignored woman artist who has now become known all over the world. Through Artemisia's story Mary illustrates for our own time the dangers of an imbalanced society, a masculine culture detrimental to the feminine.

Mary and her partner, in both senses, Norma Broude, have received many honors for their work. Colleagues at American University established a Broude-Garrard biannual conference in their honor. Members of the art department are making plans to set aside a space for a Broude-Garrard library which will one day contain books Mary and Norma plan to donate that have been essential to their work.

At this writing, Mary is eighty-five. Her life is as busy as ever, filled with publishing books and articles, giving interviews and lectures, sitting on panels, curating art exhibits, and mentoring young scholars. She's been part of the feminist movement for over fifty years. In a recent interview, a young student asked her what feminist art history was like when she was in graduate school. Mary hesitated before saying gently, "There wasn't any feminist art history when I was in graduate school." Since her accomplishments are well documented and can be found on any search engine and her books are easily acquired, I will "unveil" another side from a sister's point of view.

She was named Mary DuBose Garrard, the first and middle names after Ganny, and at my suggestion, my children and grandchildren call her May May, Ganny's nickname. Mary thinks we are both five feet tall, but the truth is I'm a half inch taller. We both have blue eyes and fair skin. Her hair is dark blonde with only a tinge of gray while mine, once light brown, is white (due only to the fact that I had children and she didn't).

She is not only brilliant but kind, loving, fun, funny, curious, humble, courageous, and compassionate. She has never thought of herself as exceptional and believes that all of us have the potential to succeed in whatever way we define success, a belief that has both goaded and challenged me.

We are very different. Unless her passion is stirred by an injustice, she takes after our mild-mannered father: I am more volatile. Our lifestyles are different. I chose to have children, she chose not to, and we deeply appreciate each other's choices. On politics and family matters, we usually agree. We both have a passion for teaching and writing, and a deep interest in people.

Mary is adept at using an online "app" for drawing, and with it she makes meaningful greetings to family and friends at Christmas and on birthdays. An ongoing project is her version of *The Odyssey* that she produces by using the same drawing app. She tells the story of Odysseus's adventures in clean, well-proportioned lines, vivid colors, and zippy captions. By the time she finishes, I suspect that Penelope will have played a much larger role than in Homer's version.

Mary has traveled widely. For her it's almost a second career. She takes frequent trips to Italy and many other places and lives part of the year in Washington, D.C., and part in Miami, Florida. Luckily for me, Mississippi is regularly on her itinerary.

When Craig and Will were growing up, she caught some of their priceless comments that Claiborne and I had missed. She overheard

Craig speak her first sentence: "Pup Pup night night." (The dog has gone to sleep.) Mary was there when Will made a remark that has become, in our common history, a much-used line. After a big Christmas dinner of turkey and tryptophan, Will wanted May May to play yet another board game. "Now?" Mary said. "Why?"

"You gotta do something," Will replied.

Always an attentive aunt to my children, she's also taken an avid interest in my grandchildren. When I took my grandson to Washington to see her and Norma, Mary drove us to all the sights and then unflaggingly made the same rounds again for my granddaughter two years later.

Though she sits at a computer for a good part of every day, Mary disclaims any knowledge as to how they work. Once she told me she'd fixed a computer glitch. When I asked her if she felt more empowered, she said, "No. Less enfeebled." Even if computers are beyond her, she's an inventor at heart. She dreamed of moving sidewalks long before anybody else. She and Claiborne once built what they called a "pop tent," a lightweight, portable apparatus to protect beachgoers from the sun, wind, and heat, only to find out that one of the outdoor companies had beat them to the patent.

Except for a two-year Covid gap, Mary and I get together at least once a year and make weekly phone calls that last at least an hour. We talk about everything: relationships, TV shows, trips, who's ahead in our games of Words with Friends, politicians good and bad, the latest appliance crisis, writers, artists, movies, her writing, my writing, what we're reading, my knee, her back, good meals, and bad. At some point, these heady discussions devolve into fits of laughter.

Together, Mary and I remember things we would have separately forgotten. Recently, I asked her if she remembered Daddy's two-way radio. We had a good laugh over that. Always a fan of cars and gadgetry, he was entranced by a two-way radio that he'd bought to communicate with his managers. "Unit One to Unit Two," he'd say importantly into the microphone even though the manager was standing only a few yards away. Then there was the night we sang all thirty miles home from a restaurant in Greenwood called Lusco's, to Claiborne's chagrin. We sang all of Mother's old favorites: "For Me and My Gal," "Harvest Moon," "You Are My Sunshine," "Don't Bring Lulu," and a dozen or thirty more.

We like to laugh over a memorable remark made by Mother's seamstress. When Mother called her and said she wanted a dress altered by Friday, Mrs. M. famously replied, "No can do. By Friday I'll be drunk and gone to Memphis."

More beautiful than all the eloquent words Mary used to write her books were the ones she spoke to Claiborne after we quit farming. He was suffering deep regret because he thought he'd let us down. "You did the best you could," she said. Plain words on a plain truth that she could see when he could not.

• • •

Before Mary left Washington for Indianola for the unveiling event, I texted her to say that if Daddy were alive, I bet he'd take his buddies by the library every day to show them her marker. She said she wasn't sure he'd get it, meaning her career. "Maybe not," I said. "But that wouldn't have stopped him from being proud."

The event on June 26 might be a good place to stop. I've come full circle, back to the place that shaped me, but did not define me. A place and people that gave rise to the full catastrophe.

I wouldn't have missed it.

Epilogue

I was about to send in the final draft of this book when Annie Chapman Collins died. It happened on February 14, 2024—Valentine's Day *and* Ash Wednesday. She was 105 years old.

According to her home health nurses and her loyal friend Genetta Ford, Annie was kind to them and everyone else to the very end. She didn't complain; she was never grouchy or irritable towards them, despite any pain or discomfort she might have felt, and yet she freely expressed what she felt—joy, sorrow, and everything in between. She kept her own counsel and sometimes didn't go along with her helpers' ideas for her care. If their plan was to bathe or feed her, she might say, "I know y'all are trying to help, but I'm not going to do that right now."

At her funeral, Reverend Turner told us what he witnessed when he was with her in the hospital on the day before she died. Though outwardly compliant and calm, she threw off her oxygen tube and heart monitor three different times as soon as the nurse left the room. "She was ready to go," he said.

I can only guess that Annie's absence of anger and fear came from an inner authority rarely seen in this world.

Addenda

Addendum A. Tribute to Anna Cannon Trice

From *A History of Northeast Mississippi* by Saville Clark (1984). Published by the author. Tupelo, Mississippi, April 11, 1919:

Professor Windham called the meeting to order and read the card of appreciation.

> For the past twenty years Tupelo has been peculiarly blessed in having at the head of the primary department of her school, Mrs. Anna Trice. And we the mothers of the city, whose children from year to year have had the advantage of being her pupils, are employing this method of expressing . . . appreciation of her noble work on behalf of our little ones. . . .
>
> We do pray that she may be spared many years to continue her work. We do thank the Giver of all good things for letting us have her for so long.
>
> Signed by over 100 women of Tupelo

Addendum B. Uncle Turner

In my uncle Saville Clark's self-published book *A History of Northeast Mississippi*, he tells a priceless yarn about the writer Andrew Lytle and the inimitable Uncle Turner Clark. Here's the excerpt:

> In Vanderbilt, I had told Andrew [Lytle] about Uncle Turner and his tales. "When I and Bedford Forrest" Andrew wrote me, asking for an introduction. I answered that no introduction was necessary; just say he was a friend of mine.
>
> A month or so later Andrew reported: As you said I probably would, I found Mr. [Turner] Clark sitting in his chair, on the shady side of the warehouse, "Mr. Clark I am a friend of Saville . . ." "Saville! A fine boy; made a crop for me once. What can I do for you, young man?"
>
> Andrew told him he was interested in any letters, papers, maps connected with General Forrest or the Battle of Harrisburg. "Papers? Maps? We don't need those things. Get in my car, young man. I'll take you to the battlefield and tell you all about it." They got in the car, a runabout with top down. Uncle Turner settled himself, started the motor, blew the horn three times, shoved the gear lever into reverse and backed into a Model-T parked behind him. Uncle Turner heaved himself around, glared at the terrified countrywoman seated in the Ford, "Great God, woman, didn't you hear me blow my horn?"
>
> They drove off and there followed, wrote Andrew, three hours of the most graphic and entertaining, and wholly inaccurate, description of the Battle of Harrisburg.

Addendum C. Lyrics to "Has Anybody Seen My Gal?"

Five foot two, eyes of blue
But oh, what those five feet could do
Has anybody seen my gal?
Turned up nose, turned down hose
Flapper yes, she's one of those
Has anybody seen my gal?

Now if you run into a
Five foot two, covered with pearls
Diamond rings and all those things
Bet your life if it isn't her
But could she love, could she woo?
Could she, could she, could she coo?
Has anybody seen my gal?

Addendum D. One Cannon's Many Priceless Letters to Ganny

March 25, 1957

San Reno, Italy

Dear Mother—

Yours written last Tues—Mar 19 came this morning & reached San Reno Saturday but evidently too late for week-end delivery. When I got here your letter dated Mar 2 was waiting, but I didn't go back to the P.O. So if you sent another letter there on the 5th just before leaving Ind. it has now been ret-d to you. Anyway I'm glad today's news about Bess is not bad. Maybe she'll have more "remissions." I hope she doesn't suffer whether she goes or not.

Have been in the Casino at Monte Carlo a couple of times. Didn't gamble though. Looks kind of dingy, though it isn't really. Monaco itself is a lovely place. Went the first time with a nice English couple in their early thirties. He told me they run an Inn in an old converted layout—16th century. I thought he said "Luxford." He said "no, Knutsford, K silent." "King Knute is supposed to have forded the stream there, which is one yard wide." That sounded kind of familiar. Then she asked if I had read Cranford by Mrs. Gaskell. Knutsford is Cranford. They said you can easily find all of the buildings and shops she [Mrs. Gaskell] talked about. They were here about a week and very pleasant company. Have 3 children but left them at home.

Have you seen the latest issue of Life with cover showing Minoan maidens? That's what I went to Crete to see—Knossos and Life comes out with that. The girl on the right is obviously inspired by a beautiful little mural fragment in the Museum at Herakleon–a girl's head that the workmen nick-named "La Parisienne." At the end of the article the museum director, Mr. Platon, is mentioned. I had met an archaeologist, and he told me. Mr. Platon got me started in it and said "When you come back to Herakleon I want to take you up on Mt. Ida and show you the cave where Zeus was born." Prices in Greece & Crete are much lower than Italy & the Greeks are very kind and very keen minded too—Good people.

Went over to the French Riviera this week-end—along the middle-Corniche Road—the scenic & came back the Corniche Littorel—much more interesting & livable. The hostess on the bus going over was very nice & showed me everything—famous villas & historical places. The fort where Napoleon was commissioned sub-lieut. Of Artillery; where he landed at Golfe Juan on escape from Elba; Roman Theatre at Ventimiglia; villas of Churchill, Duke of Windsor, Rudolf Valentino, (now Warner Bros), Aly Khan, Rita Hayworth, Fernandel, King Farouk, Eden Roe & many others.

She knew the Roman History thoroughly. Just several people on the bus, so the driver weaved off his course & stopped everywhere the girl told him. What people! They enjoy it if the passengers do.

Leaving in the morning for Verona via Milan. Then into France some way, maybe via Innsbruck. I'll try to catch Mary somewhere on the itinerary you sent.

I'm glad Saville's back is better. I imagine after you reach field grade the back isn't so important though.

Yesterday's paper says some sharp quakes in the Bay Area of San Fran—I always miss out. Aetna was puffing when I was in Taormina & 2 days after I left it boiled up & chased the villagers down. They say it's going to erupt soon. Right after I left Greece they had the bad quakes there. I'm not causing them but would like to be around sometime—in safety, of course—

I'll send you a picture of Juliet's tomb from Verona—The best I can tell you from here is to write Mon or Tues—Apr 1 or 2 to:

Thos Cook & Son
No 2 Place de la Madeleine
Paris, France
After that wait for later advice.

Wish I could have been there to see Bill Jr with you. As a Tupeloan can't you line him up to do some arrangements for Elvis Presley? Seriously I'd like to hear some of his work—Will you see Ann & Fay this trip. I see Easter is Apr 21 this year.

I'm going over to Cook's & get my tickets etc. then back. Go by bus to Milan—and by sail to Innsbruck, through the Brenner Pass. Will be in V. at least 3 days. Its only 50 minutes by hourly buses to Sarmione on Lake Garda Pass. That's where Catullus' Villa "Sirmic–the almost island" was so will go there. Also probably run over to Venice if I feel like it. Somehow Venice doesn't appeal to me much—not as it did when I read "Marietta, a Maid of Venice" & Zoy's the glass-blower, her hero.

I imagine you are enjoying the azaleas & other blooms at C.J. [Camp Le Jeune]—or did when you first got there. Hope all is good as can expect when I got your last letter.

Love, C

Addendum E. Wheeler Parker

Parker has recently published his autobiography, *A Few Days Full of Trouble: Revelations on the Journey to Justice for my Cousin and Best Friend, Emmett Till.*

Notes

Chapter 3. Her Legacy

1. James Trice Jr., geni.com. www.geni.com-people-James-Trice-Jr.

Chapter 6. Gandaddy Clark

1. "New President of Land Bank Is Chosen." *The Times-Picayune*, Saturday, January 10, 1931, n.p.

2. "A Door to Greater Usefulness." Quoted in *The Tupelo Daily News*, 4, n.d.

Chapter 9. Garrard Forebears

1. Anna Russell Des Cognets, *Governor Garrard of Kentucky and His Descendants* (Lexington, KY, James M. Byrnes,1898).

2. Des Cognets, 16.

Chapter 10. At Rosemary

1. Mary Jayne Garrard Whittington, *Reveille: Selected Memories of a WAC*. Printed by the author, 2003, 4–5.

2. Noel Workman, *Staplcotn: The First 75 Years* (Jackson, MS: Hederman Brothers printing, 1996), 12–13.

3. Workman, 13.

4. Workman, 4–5.

5. Workman, 56.

6. Mary Jayne Whittington, "From the Delta." *The Delta Review*, August 1968, 67.

7. Mabelle G. White, "Par for the Old Course." *The Delta Review*, April/May 1965, 46.

Chapter 11. Those Absent

1. James Moseley Garrard, *Allegiance: World War II Letters Home*. Eds. Mary Jayne Garrard Whittington and Mabelle Garrard White. (Greenwood, MS: Baff Printing Company, 1990.)

2. Garrard, 40.

3. "For Them That Died in Battle," in *The Collected Poems of William Alexander Percy*, foreword by Roark Bradford. (New York, Alfred A. Knopf, 1915), 196.

Chapter 14. Love Letters

1. "Miss Lucile Clark is Married to Mr. Garrard." *The Birmingham News*, July 1, 1934, 21.

2. Lynne F. White, *Middlegate: A Japanese Garden*. Preface. Privately published; city not noted, 2011.

Chapter 15. The Delta, Part One

1. William Alexander Percy, *Lanterns on the Levee* (New York: Alfred A. Knopf, 1959), 3.

2. Percy, 129.

3. Percy, 15.

4. Walker Percy, *The Last Gentleman* (New York: Farrar, Straus and Giroux, 1966), 303.

5. David Cohn, *Where I Was Born and Raised* (Notre Dame—London: University of Notre Dame Press, 1935), 12.

6. Willie Morris, *North Toward Home* (Boston: Houghton Mifflin Company, 1967), 3–4.

Chapter 16. The Delta, Part Two

1. John Dollard, *Caste and Class in a Southern Town* (Garden City, NY: Doubleday Anchor Books, 1937).

2. Hortense Powdermaker, *After Freedom* (New York: Atheneum, 1968).

3. Powdermaker, 329.

4, Powdermaker, 328.

5. Powdermaker, 330.

6. Powdermaker, 351–52.

Chapter 17. "Nothing Gold Can Stay"

1. Robert Frost, "Nothing Gold Can Stay." https://www.poetryfoundation.org.

Chapter 18. On Barberry Lane

1. Carl Jung, The *Collected Works* (New York: Princeton University Press, 1954), 78.

Chapter 23. Cathedral Days

1. "60 Years since James Meredith Enrolled at Ole Miss," clarionledger.com, https://www.clarionledger.com/story/news/2022/09/27/60years.

Chapter 25. Why Did She Stay?

1. Joshua Liebman, *Peace of Mind* (New York: Simon and Schuster, 1946), 109.

2. James Hollis, *Swamplands of the Soul* (Toronto: Inner City Books, 1996), 93.

Chapter 29. Endings, Beginnings

1. Richo, David, *Shadow Dance* (Boston: Shambala Publications, Inc., 1999), 170.

Chapter 33. The Delta, Part Three

1. Robert Palmer, "At Mississippi Homecoming, B.B. King Unites Neighbors," nytimes.com, https://www.nytimes.com/1983/06/11arts/at-mississipppi-homecoming-bb-king-units-neighbors.html.

2. Ed Rabel, "Indianola, Mississippi," *CBS Sunday Morning* with Diane Sawyer, July 17, 1983.

Chapter 34. Dorothy

1. Martin LaBorde, *The Magic Book of Bodo* (New Orleans: Creative Endeavors Publications, 1998), n.p.

2. LaBorde, n.p.

Chapter 36. The Unveiling

1. Barbara J. Love, ed. *Feminists Who Changed America* 1963–1975 (Urbane: University of Illinois Press, 2006), 168.

Bibliography

Cohn, David. *Where I Was Born and Raised.* Notre Dame—London: University of Notre Dame Press, 1935.

Des Cognets, Anna Russell. *Governor Garrard of Kentucky and His Descendants.* Lexington, KY: James M. Byrnes, 1898.

Dollard, John. *Caste and Class in a Southern Town.* Garden City, New York: Doubleday Anchor Books, 1937.

"A Door to Greater Usefulness," *The Tupelo Daily News*, 4, n.d.

Frost, Robert. "Nothing Gold Can Stay." https://www.poetryfoundation.org.

Garrard, James Moseley. *Allegiance: World War II Letters Home.* Eds. Mary Jayne Garrard Whittington and Mabelle Garrard White. Greenwood, MS: Baff Printing Co., 1990.

Hollis, James. *Swamplands of the Soul.* Toronto: Inner City Books, 1996.

Jung, Carl. *The Collected Works*, vol. 17, 78. New York: Princeton University Press, 1954.

LaBorde, Martin. *The Magic Book of Bodo.* New Orleans: Creative Endeavors Publications, 1998.

Liebman, Joshua Loth. *Peace of Mind.* New York: Simon and Schuster, 1946. Reprinted by Simon and Schuster, August 26, 1998.

Love, Barbara J., ed. *Feminists Who Changed America 1963–1975.* Urbane: University of Illinois Press, 2006, 168.

"Miss Lucile Clark Is Married to Mr. Garrard," *The Birmingham News*, Sunday, July 1, 1934.

Morris, Willie. *North Toward Home.* Boston: Houghton Mifflin Company, 1967.

"New President of Land Bank Is Chosen," *The Times-Picayune*, Saturday, January 10, 1931.

The Oxford Language Dictionary. https://languages.oup.com.

Percy, Walker. *The Last Gentleman.* New York: Farrar, Straus and Giroux, 1966.

Percy, William Alexander. "For Them That Died in Battle" in *The Collected Poems of William Alexander Percy.* New York: Alfred A. Knopf, 1915.

Percy, William Alexander. *Lanterns on the Levee.* New York: Alfred A. Knopf, 1959.

Powdermaker, Hortense. *After Freedom.* New York: Atheneum, 1968.

Richo, David. *Shadow Dance.* Boston: Shambala Publications, 1999.

"60 Years since James Meredith Enrolled at Ole Miss," clarionledger.com, September 27, 2022.

Trice, James, Jr. "Genealogy of the Trice Family from the Seventeenth Century." www.geni.com-people-James-Trice-Jr.

White, Lynne F. *Middlegate: A Japanese Garden.* Privately published, 2011.

White, Mabelle G. "Par for the Old Course." *The Delta Review*, April/May 1965, 46.

Whittington, Mary Jayne Garrard. *Reveille: The Selected Memories of a WAC.* Printed by the author, 2003.

Whittington, Mary Jayne Garrard. "From the Delta," *The Delta Review*, August 1968, 67.

Workman, Noel. *Staplcotn: The First 75 Years.* Jackson, MS: Hederman Brothers, 1996.

About the Author

Photo courtesy of the author

Marion Garrard Barnwell taught literature and writing courses at Delta State University in Cleveland, Mississippi, for twenty-five years. She cofounded *Tapestry*, a literary magazine for faculty at Delta State. She compiled and edited *A Place Called Mississippi*, which won a Special Achievement Award from the Mississippi Institute of Arts and Letters. Barnwell coauthored *Touring Literary Mississippi* with Patti Carr Black and helped coedit *Fannye Cook: Mississippi's Pioneering Conservationist* after the death of author, Dorothy Shawhan. Barnwell's short fiction has been collected in *Mad Dogs and Moonshine*, *Christmas Stories from Mississippi*, *What Would Elvis Think?*, and *On the Way Home*.